THE ART OF
PRACTICAL
SPIRITUALITY

THE ART OF
PRACTICAL
SPIRITUALITY

*How to Bring More Passion, Creativity
and Balance into Everyday Life*

ELIZABETH CLARE PROPHET
WITH PATRICIA R. SPADARO

SUMMIT UNIVERSITY PRESS®
Corwin Springs, Montana

THE ART OF PRACTICAL SPIRITUALITY
How to Bring More Passion, Creativity
and Balance into Everyday Life
by Elizabeth Clare Prophet with Patricia R. Spadaro
Copyright © 2000 by Summit University Press
All rights reserved

Library of Congress Catalog Card Number: 99-69972
ISBN: 0-922729-55-7

SUMMIT UNIVERSITY ♆ PRESS®

Summit University Press and ♆ are registered trademarks.

Printed in the United States of America
05 04 03 02 01   6 5 4 3 2

Contents

CONTENTS

Note: Because gender-neutral language can be cumbersome and at times confusing, we have used *he* and *him* to refer to God or the individual and *mankind* to refer to people in general. These terms are for readability only and are not intended to exclude women or the feminine aspect of the Godhead, just as our use of the term *God* is not meant to exclude other expressions for the Divine.

Everyday Spirituality

*"What is the path?" the Zen master
Nan-sen was asked. "Everyday
life is the path," he answered.*

At one time or another we have
all had a peak spiritual experience, whether
we've called it that or not. Maybe it was a profound sense of inner peace or a deep communion with nature. Maybe it happened during a
long trek into the mountains or when you first
fell in love. But that feeling, whatever it was,
just didn't last long enough, and you were left
wondering how to recapture the moment.

How do we sustain that inner peace? How
do we endow our relationships, our family life

and our work with a spiritual spark? How do we tap our inner resources to handle stress and overcome the blocks to our creativity? How do we make our spirituality practical?

I've been pursuing the art of practical spirituality all my life. I can't remember a time when I wasn't walking and talking with God. As a child, my spiritual quest took me to all the churches and the synagogue in my hometown. Later, I took up the study of the world's religions.

Ultimately, my search brought me to the feet of the great luminaries known as the ascended masters—the saints and adepts who have emerged out of the spiritual traditions of East and West. These enlightened ones have fulfilled their reason for being and "ascended," or become one with God. Each one has something uniquely compelling to teach us about the art of practical spirituality.

I don't believe that any one person or spiritual tradition has a corner on spirituality but that we can learn something from everyone.

Just as there are many ways to climb a mountain, so there are many ways to climb to the summit of being. Each path gives you a different perspective of that summit—a new way of understanding who God is and who you are.

We are climbing that mountain every day, not just when we're taking time out to meditate in the mountains or watch a beautiful sunset. Spirituality is an everyday affair.

A Working Relationship with Spirit

What does it mean to live a spiritual life, and what is spirituality? The word *spirit* comes from the Latin *spiritus,* meaning "breath," "breath of a god," or "inspiration." Spirituality is to the soul what the breath of life is to a newborn child. Spirituality infuses you with life. It gives you peace and purpose. It empowers you to love and nourish yourself and others.

Spirituality is being able to sustain a working relationship with Spirit. It doesn't matter whether you call that spiritual fount the Christ or the Buddha, the Tao or Brahman. We can all get in touch—and stay in touch—with the universal power of Spirit by working with that relationship, making that connection, every day.

When we talk about practical spirituality, we're really talking about spiritual empowerment, the power to transform ourselves and the world around us. Spiritual empowerment starts with understanding: *Who am I and why am I here? Where am I going and how do I get there?*

Who Am I?

You are a spiritual being—a child of God clothed with human form and personality. You have a divine nature, and a part of God resides deep within you. This is your personal source of power.

Hindu tradition mysteriously describes this indwelling spirit as "the inmost Self, no bigger than a thumb" who "lives in the heart." Buddhists call it the Buddha nature. Jewish mystics refer to it as the neshamah. Fourteenth-century

Christian theologian and mystic Meister Eckhart claimed that "God's seed is within us." There is a part of us, he wrote, that "remains eternally in the Spirit and is divine.... Here God glows and flames without ceasing."

Though they approach it from different angles, all of these mystical paths are describing the spiritual flame, the divine spark, that pulsates in the inner recesses of your heart. Some people who have heard me teach this concept over the years have had a hard time accepting that a part of God lives inside of them. That's because many of us were taught as children to look outside of ourselves for the solutions to life's problems rather than to access the spiritual power within to meet those challenges.

I like the way the ancients explained it. Both Buddhists and the early Christians known as gnostics[1] used the image of the "gold in the mud" to help people understand their spiritual essence. They said the gold of our spirit may be covered over by the mud of the world, but the mud never destroys that innate spirit.

In other words, it doesn't matter what you've been through. It doesn't matter how much mud has splattered onto your spirit and shaped your outer personality as you've trudged through the trenches of life. It doesn't matter what other people say about you. You still have a beautiful, everlasting spark of God right inside of you.

In addition to your divine spark, another component of your reality is your Higher Self. Your Higher Self is your wise inner self, your chief guardian angel, your dearest friend. Jesus discovered the Higher Self to be "the Christ" and Gautama discovered it to be "the Buddha," and thus that Higher Self is also called the inner Christ (or Christ Self) and the inner Buddha. Christian mystics sometimes refer to it as the inner man of the heart or the Inner Light.

Your Higher Self is your inner teacher whose still small voice speaks within you— warning you of danger, teaching you, calling you back to the point of your divine reality. Your Higher Self will always give you unerring direction, if you will take the time to tune into that voice. As Mahatma Gandhi once said, "The only tyrant I accept in this world is the 'still small voice' within."

Why Am I Here and Where Am I Going?

The goal for each of us is to be, right here on earth, the reflection of our Higher Self—to manifest the full potential inherent in our spiritual self. That's what Gautama Buddha did and that's why he is called the "Buddha" (meaning "awakened one"). That's what Jesus did and that's why he is called the "Christ" (meaning "anointed"), the one anointed with the light of that Higher Self. Because Jesus fully embodied his Higher Self, the apostle Paul said, "In him dwelleth all the fullness of the Godhead bodily."

Gautama Buddha, Jesus and all the ascended masters tell us that we, too, can realize our full spiritual potential. How? By understanding, accessing and developing the spiritual part of ourselves. By liberating our own inner greatness so that we can fulfill our soul's highest calling and help others do the same.

We all have moments when we feel connected with our Higher Self—when we are creative and sensitive, compassionate and caring, loving and joyful. But there are other moments when we feel out of sync with our Higher Self—moments when we become angry, depressed, lost. What the spiritual path is all about is learning to sustain the connection to the higher part of ourselves so that we can make our greatest contribution to humanity.

How Do I Get There?

Step by step, your soul is learning to access her inner power in order to fulfill the destiny that is uniquely yours. This doesn't happen all at once. It happens a little bit every day. Spirituality is a process—a path. We're not only walking that path; sometimes we're putting it together as we go. And it's not just *what* we do as we take this journey but *how* we do it.

In the process of walking your own path and fulfilling your destiny, do you endow your actions and all of your relationships—at home, at work, at play—with the special quality of heart that only you can give? Are you able to stay connected with that spiritual part of yourself? Are you able to dip deeply into your divine nature to uplift those you interact with? This is the fine art of practical spirituality. "To affect the quality of the day," said Thoreau, "that is the highest of arts."

On a very practical level, people often ask me: How can I handle the stresses of daily life and still keep my spiritual attunement? How can I be spiritual when my computer just crashed—for the fifth time today? Or when I have to work late again and my seven-year-old is expecting me to show up for his soccer game? Or when I just found out that management is downsizing? How can I find inner peace when there is turmoil all around me?

It isn't easy. But there are practical spiritual solutions to today's challenges. There are maps that can help us navigate through the rough seas and narrow straits of life. That's what the rest of this book is all about.

The keys to practical spirituality on the following pages are gleaned from the ancient wisdom of the world's spiritual traditions as well as practical experience. They have helped me and many others as we have applied them to the challenges of daily life. What I've shared here is foundational but by no means exhaustive. There is so much more that could be said—and each key could be the subject of a book in itself. In fact, this is just the beginning. The ending, after all, is up to us.

Discover your soul's core passion and shape it into a mission

Each man has his own vocation....
There is one direction in which
all space is open to him.

—RALPH WALDO EMERSON

You were born with a unique purpose to fulfill on earth. That means there is something that is yours, and yours alone, to do—and unless you do it for loved ones or for the betterment of mankind, no one will.

Many of us don't have the faintest idea what our mission is, or even that we're supposed to have one. To find your mission, start by asking yourself: *What am I passionate about?*

What is it that I love to do, that I live just to do?
Plain and simple, what makes me happy?

A Hasidic saying advises, "Everyone should carefully observe which way his heart draws him, and then choose that way with all his strength." You will know your passion because it makes your heart sing. It's the thing that gets you out of bed in the morning. When you talk about it, you become spirited, energized, alive.

That doesn't mean, however, that pursuing your soul's passion will always be easy. It can feel like both the agony and the ecstasy. For one thing, you may have to fend off the raucous voices that will try as hard as they can to drown out the voice of your soul.

T. S. Eliot once gave this advice to students: "Whatever you think, be sure it is what you think. . . . It is bad enough to think and want the things that your elders want you to think and want, but it is still worse to think and want just like all your contemporaries." And Bertrand Russell once quipped, "One should respect public opinion insofar as it is necessary to avoid starvation and keep out of prison."

Another reason following your life's passion isn't always easy is that it takes hard work. Our calling is the crucible in which we forge our true identity. It's the laboratory where we, like alchemists of the spirit, learn to transform the base metals of our lower nature into the gold of our highest self. This soul work is a sacred

> *May you live every day of your life.*
> —JONATHAN SWIFT

labor that we undertake not only for ourselves but for others. What will come out of it is a gift that we can lay on the altar of humanity.

If we don't accept the challenge, if we decide to take the easy way out—because it's more comfortable or lucrative—then we've betrayed our own soul. For the soul, as Jim Lehrer once observed, "must be nourished along with the bank account and the resumé."

Sometimes we do have obligations to others that prevent us from immediately pursuing our passion to the fullest. Some of these obligations may stem from our karma.[2] For instance, circumstances may demand that for a season you must care for a child or an ailing parent or support someone else at the expense of your own desires.

It is always important to tend to karmic obligations, but once you have paid off these spiritual "debts" to others you will feel much lighter and your soul will be free to pursue its highest calling. The best way to free yourself from a limiting karmic circumstance is to pour yourself wholeheartedly and joyfully into fulfilling that obligation so you can get through it and move on.

Another principle to remember is that your mission is not necessarily equal to your job. It's wonderful if you are able to mold your passion into a career, but your mission doesn't have to be what you do for a living. It may be something you do after work hours, like composing music or working with disadvantaged children or taking care of animals.

In fact, your mission may not be what you

do at all, but what you *are*. Your mission may be to bring into your interactions with others, into your relationships, into everything you do a singular spiritual quality (like love, compassion, patience, truthfulness) so that your very life is an example to others.

For example, Mother Teresa's calling, and that of her Missionaries of Charity, was to serve the poorest of the poor while living among them. But it was more than that. Her mission was to be love in action. "We have to bring God's love to the people by our service," Mother Teresa once said. "We do no great things, only small things with great love."

The ascended master El Morya, known to students of Theosophy as the Master M., says our mission involves perfecting the talents that God has placed within our soul. God has given you certain talents so that you can share the highest and truest part of yourself with others. "The purpose of life," he says, "is to find God—in yourself, in your talents, in your calling and in your sacred labor. It is to endow anything that you do with his Spirit."

In the most popular spiritual classic of India, the Bhagavad Gita, the hero Krishna counsels his disciple and friend Arjuna to fulfill his *dharma,* the divine plan for his soul. Our dharma is our reason for being—our duty to be who we really are, to fulfill our true potential.

The purpose of life is a life of purpose.

—ROBERT BYRNE

When on the eve of a crucial battle the warrior Arjuna hesitates, Krishna teaches him, "One's own dharma, even when not done perfectly, is better than someone else's dharma, even though well performed."

This profound teaching drives home the point that it is your spiritual duty to pursue your own mission. El Morya puts it this way: "One's own canoe, though full of holes, is better than another's ship. We value sailing only in one's own boat."

When we do not pursue our soul's passion, the consequences can be spiritually, emotionally and even physically devastating. Not only can it make us grouchy, but it can make us emotionally and physically ill. "The lost soul," writes medical intuitive Caroline Myss, "is very susceptible to illness."[3]

The feeling that life has lost its soul, or that our soul has lost its life, can also lead to addictions as a way to escape from reality. From a spiritual standpoint, it can lead to a dark night of the soul.

I encourage you to set aside time when you are by yourself to consider the following questions. They are some of the most important questions you will ever answer in this life. In fact, we periodically need to ask ourselves these questions because as our soul develops, our mission does too.

Spiritual Exercises

■ **Discover your passion.** If you have never thought about your passion in life, answering these questions may not be easy. Just let your heart speak to you and allow the answers to come in their own time. Ask your Higher Self to send you divine direction, and then be open to all possibilities.

Am I happy with the direction of my life and with how I spend most of my time?

What is my passion in life?

What is the greatest talent God has given me to share with others?

How can I refine it and perfect it?

*How can I use my talent to make the
most outstanding contribution to my family,
my community, those who need me
in my circle of influence?*

*How can I capitalize on this talent
to make a living and thus devote a major
percentage of my time to it?*

2 Simplify and focus by prioritizing both material and spiritual goals

*In the long run men hit only
what they aim at.*

— HENRY DAVID THOREAU

Today, in an age of increasing complexity, speed and pressure, many are opting for simpler lifestyles. They are trading in the exhausting climb up the corporate ladder for greater personal freedom, more time with family and friends, and less stressful jobs—even if they pay less.

The Trends Research Institute of Rhinebeck, New York, estimates that 15 percent of American adults have adopted a downscaled lifestyle, and by 2005 at least 15 percent of the developed world will be practicing voluntary simplicity in some form (up from less than 2 percent in 1998). This is not just another fad. It is an entire generation's response to the soul's deep yearning for a more direct and meaningful approach to life.

Simplifying our lifestyles can only come once we have figured out what our priorities are—not just our material goals but our spiritual ones too. The answer will be different for each of us. We all need different material and spiritual supports to help us reach our destination. But if you feel you're being forced to run faster than your legs will carry you, it may be time to sit down and reassess priorities.

Have you taken time lately to seriously consider: *What are my specific goals for my career, my relationships, my health, my home, my family life, my spiritual life?*

In terms of spiritual goals, ask yourself not only *what you want to do* but also *what you want to be*. For instance, how much time do you want to spend meditating, self-reflecting, journaling, volunteering in your local community? Also take a good look at what you want to become and what it will take to get there. Do you want to become more patient? more intuitive? more compassionate? What are the stumbling blocks to that spiritual growth? What do you need to do to resolve the anger or the pride or the anxiety that keeps getting in your way?

A good way to begin to simplify and focus on your goals is to *write down the goals you want to accomplish in each department of your life. Then, drawing from your entire list, rank your goals from the most important to the least important. Next, ask yourself how much time you spend on your top three goals.*

Those who compare their top goals to what they actually spend most of their time doing are often surprised to see that they are spending little or no time at all on what they value most. If the amount of time you spend on your top goals is out of sync with their priority in your life, then you know that something has to change.

But don't stop there. The next step is one of the most important. Ask yourself: *What am I doing now that isn't contributing to my top goals? What do I spend my time doing that isn't moving me forward?*

> *To nourish the heart there is nothing better than to make the desires few.*
>
> —MENCIUS

To take a simple example, if you spend ten hours a week watching TV and two hours going to a movie but you aren't nurturing your soul by writing the poetry you've promised yourself, you might consider reorganizing your weeknights or weekends. If the three hours you spend cleaning your home each week is time you'd rather spend reading or taking a yoga class or leading a local youth group, you might consider hiring someone to help with the household chores.

This exercise sounds simplistic, but it is profound. Some of the running around in circles we do is simply because we don't stop to figure out our real priorities and then focus on them. Or we focus on material goals only, when in reality our spiritual goals require just as much, if not more, attention.

It's a good idea to repeat this exercise and revisit your list of goals periodically because your priorities may change as your direction and values evolve or become clearer.

Spiritual Exercises ────────────

■ **Prioritize.** Take some time to go through the steps for prioritizing spiritual and material goals, outlined in italics on pages 21–23.

■ **Be true to yourself.** Making the best use of your time and energy is a daily decision. Try taking time every Sunday evening, before the start of your week, to answer this one question: *What are the most important things I could be doing this week to bring me closer to achieving the top three priorities in my life?*

Even though you will have plenty of other obligations to fulfill during the week, schedule time into your days to be true to yourself.

3 Listen within for the voice of wisdom

Can you be still and look inside? If so, then you will see that the truth is always available, always responsive.

— LAO TZU

The still small voice within us is speaking, but we're not always listening. The art of practical spirituality involves keeping one ear inclined to our duties on earth and one ear attuned to the inner voice of wisdom that is trying, sometimes desperately, to get our attention.

That inner voice can come to us as direction from our Higher Self or a signal from our soul. It can be the nudge of an angel or the message of a master. But if we constantly surround ourselves with noise—whether it's music or TV or phone conversations—we may be drowning out the valuable voices of the spirit that tend our soul.

Brother Lawrence, a seventeenth-century monk, made the art of listening the centerpiece of his spiritual path. He called it the practice of the presence of God. Brother Lawrence said he liked to keep a "simple attentiveness and a loving gaze upon God," even midst the noise and clatter of the kitchen where he worked. He described this practice as a "habitual, silent and secret conversation of the soul with God." In other words, God is with us everywhere, not just when we're meditating or walking in nature or attending a weekend retreat. We just have to tune in.

Radio stations are always broadcasting, but unless we turn on the radio and tune in to the right frequency, we don't hear the broadcast. Well, God is like a radio station. God is everywhere we are, ready and willing to help us. We just have to tune in to the right spiritual frequency.

Rabbi Adin Steinsaltz says that in Hasidic tradition "the voice giving the Law, the Ten Commandments, never stopped.... There is a very clear message that is always being transmitted. The thing that has changed is that we are no longer listening."[4] Some of us, he admits, are just not willing to hear what God has to say. Is it because we're afraid he'll ask us to do something we don't want to do?

We can learn much about the art of listening from the mystics of the world's spiritual traditions. Tibet's great yogi Milarepa is characteristically portrayed with his right hand cupped to his ear. Scholars have surmised that he is listening to the echoes of nature or that he is a *shravaka*. The word literally means "listening to," but is used to describe a disciple of the Buddha, one who has learned to listen to the inner voice and the voice of his spiritual mentors.

In the third century, the renowned Christian theologian and mystic Origen of Alexandria taught, "Do not think that God speaks to us from outside. For those holy thoughts that arise in our heart, they are the way God speaks to us."

Mother Teresa of Calcutta talked about hearing a distinct call from God at the start of her mission. It happened while she was in quiet, intimate prayer as she was traveling on a train to Darjeeling, India. "The message was quite clear: I was to leave the convent and help the poor whilst living among them," she said. "It was an order."

Swami Prabhavananda said that his spiritual teacher once told him that he would never do anything until he was directed by God to do so. "The devotees insist upon fixing some date for my going," he said. "To avoid constant pestering I fix a tentative date. But I do not move, or do anything, until I know the will of the Lord.... Everything I do I have the direct guidance of God."[5]

The sixteenth-century mystic Teresa of Avila said her life was guided by the directions, revelations and rebukes she received from God. When God wants the soul to know something, she said, he often makes it known "without image or explicit words." Thérèse of Lisieux said the same thing, admitting that although she never heard Jesus speak to her, "he is within me at each moment; he is guiding and inspiring me with what I must say and do." Most often, she said, these moments of illumination came to her not when she was in prayer but "in the midst of my daily occupations."

She too was practicing what Brother Lawrence described as the soul's habitual, silent and secret conversation with God. The word *conversation* is key here. When we converse, we don't just talk; we also listen. "The art of conversation consists of the exercise of two fine qualities," Benjamin Disraeli once wrote. "You must possess at the same time the habit of communicating and the

> *Without even opening your window, you can know the ways of Heaven. You see: the further away you go, the less you know.*
>
> —LAO TZU

habit of listening. The union is rather rare, but irresistible."

The same two habits apply to our conversations with God—and those who are most highly attuned to that inner voice of wisdom have indeed achieved something rare but irresistible. We call them mystics or geniuses and relegate them to another category of evolution. Yet what they have done, we are all meant to do.

Like other mystics, Teresa did not think that receiving communications from God was only for a chosen few. She said the personal and direct encounter with God could take place as we go about our day-to-day business. "The Lord," she once told the sisters of her convent, "walks among the pots and pans, helping you both interiorly and exteriorly."

In her droll style, Teresa tells of a time when Jesus illumined her on a certain matter. "Soon afterward I forgot," she writes. "And while trying to recall it I heard this: 'You already know I sometimes speak to you; don't neglect to write down what I say; for even though it may not benefit you, it can benefit others.'"[6] This shows us that we have a responsibility to be attentive to the inner guidance we receive in our heart of hearts because it may save not only ourselves but others.

Teresa's inner promptings warned her of coming events and often impelled her to go against her better judgment or change plans she had already made. Yet she never regretted following the instruction she was given. She wrote that at times "the Lord warns me of some dangers I'm in, or of other persons, and about things of the future—three or four years in advance very often—all of which have been fulfilled."[7]

I have had many experiences where the voice of wisdom speaking within has given me inner guidance—direction I have always been grateful for. That direction can be extremely precise. Once I was riding in a car in the Virginia countryside. It was a magnificent day and the windows were rolled down. Suddenly I got the prompting to close my window. Just as I rolled it up a tomato splattered on it. Some children had been hiding in the bushes and throwing rotten tomatoes at cars passing by.

A friend of mine told me that one day as she was going to bed she had the feeling she should turn around and lie with her head at the foot of her bed. She didn't know why she should do this, but she decided to obey the inner voice. No sooner had she rearranged herself than her roommate's hanging plant fell off its hook and landed right where her head would have been.

I'll never forget the news story about the Seattle city bus carrying holiday shoppers that crashed through a bridge guardrail and plunged some 50 feet when the driver was shot in the arm. The bus hit the roof of an apartment complex.

A woman living there was standing outside her apartment at the time. She heard a bang and then saw concrete flying everywhere. "I just thought—I'm going to die now, I'm going to die," she said. It was then that she sensed the inner voice. "I totally froze and something like a guardian angel or something made me move." Making it out of harm's way just in time, she was only grazed by a falling piece of concrete.

God sends us messages and warnings in many ways, messages about both the big and little things in life. The inner voice of wisdom can come at any time, as long as we are open to hearing it.

It is in the silence of the heart that God speaks.

—MOTHER TERESA

So much of our day is spent in an active mode—expending energy to get things done—that we don't always take a moment to consciously move into a receptive mode. Sometimes this takes shutting out the noise of the world and moving out of the way of the people, places and circumstances that are not conducive to our ongoing communion with that inner voice. "God said it is not good for man to be alone," John Barrymore once joked, "but sometimes it is a great relief!" On a more serious note, Mother Teresa believed that it is when we are alone with God in silence that "we

accumulate the inward power which we dis-
tribute in action."

It's important to take a few moments each
day to go within to garner that inward power—
to listen for the direction, guidance and comfort
we do not always find in friend or family or
partner. It doesn't seem very hard to do—to just
stop for a moment to converse with God or our
Higher Self and then listen for the return cur-
rent. Like anything else, it's a matter of making
it a habit so that it becomes second nature.

Spiritual Exercises

■ **Enter the secret chamber and ask for divine direction.** Pause at a certain point in your day and ask God, your Higher Self, your guardian angel a question: *What direction should I take in this situation? How can I help a loved one who is hurting? How can I get past this problem that is hanging on?*

Close your eyes and see yourself entering the secret chamber of your heart, where you come face-to-face with your Higher Self. Consciously move into a receptive mode and affirm that you are open to receive the answer to your heart's prayer.

I am open to hear, sense, feel, intuit
the inner wisdom that is mine to glean.
Show me, O God, how to keep a listening ear
and an open heart and how to use the
wisdom you give me to help others.

Then listen for the answer, which may come right away or later. Be ready to receive the message and the messenger—through an inner prompting, an unexpected phone call, the unfolding of events.

■ **Schedule alone time into your week** (block it off on your daily planner if you need to)—time reserved for a longer period of conversation and communion with the divine. You can use this time to meditate or pray or read something inspirational.

■ **Savor the interludes of silence.** Avoid the temptation to fill every spare moment with the radio, TV or even music. When there is silence, savor it. These are golden opportunities to go within.

■ **Get inspired.** Take your favorite sacred text or inspirational book in your hands. Say a prayer to God to show you the answer to a question and guide you to the page that will give you what you need to hear right now. Open the book and let your eyes fall upon a particular passage.

■ **Keep a record** of the inner promptings, directions or messages you receive as you listen within for the voice of wisdom. Write down how this guidance has helped you. Then when you are going through a rough time, you can reread it to remind yourself not to lose faith in the inner voice.

■ **Share.** Like Teresa of Avila, we may have inner revelations that can benefit others. Go out of your way to share these experiences with someone who needs your help.

Create a sacred space and make a spiritual connection each morning

Your sacred space is where you can find yourself again and again.

—JOSEPH CAMPBELL

We have access to vast spiritual reserves that can guide us daily in practical ways, but we have to make the time to tap into those wellsprings of wisdom.

Many people find that creating a sacred space helps them make this connection. You can do this simply and easily by setting up your personal altar in your home, even if it's in a corner of the bedroom.

You can adorn this altar with whatever

inspires you and helps you make that connection with God and with your Higher Self. You can place candles, flowers or plants on the altar. You can add pictures or statues of saints or masters as well as photographs of those for whom you regularly pray. Beautiful crystals and a crystal bowl or goblet can serve as chalices to focus God's light in your home. Above your altar or on it, you can place the Chart of Your Divine Self[8] to help you attune with the presence of God within.

Your altar is the place you go to "alter," or transform. When I take time first thing in the morning to connect with God through heartfelt prayer, I find that my day is transformed. It goes much more smoothly. I don't get caught up in needless distractions and emergencies that pull me away from my goals.

Prayer, in reality, is a conversation. We don't just reach out to God; God also reaches out to us with guidance, comfort, direction and help. Making a spiritual connection through prayer is what Teresa of Avila called "an intimate sharing

between friends." Friends can pour out their
hearts to each other without holding back,
sharing their joys and their sorrows. We can do
the same with God in prayer. Teresa also
warned that just as "family ties and friendship
are lost through a lack of communication," our
relationship with God can be lost if we don't
pray.[9]

Your morning conversation with God
doesn't have to take long. You can sit or stand
before your altar, close your eyes, take some
deep breaths and enter into the sacred space
within your heart—the secret chamber where
your divine spark abides. Teresa of Avila called
this special place the interior castle. In Hindu
tradition, the devotee visualizes a jeweled island
in the heart, and there at his own inner altar
he pays homage to his teacher.

Jesus also spoke of that secret chamber
when he said we should go into our "closets" to
pray. When I was a little girl I kept wondering,
what kind of closets did the disciples go into?
Did people even have closets in those days? You

can't pray in a closet—there isn't enough air in there! Later I realized that going into our closet to pray is a metaphor for going into another compartment of consciousness. It's entering into that inner sanctuary of the heart and closing the door on the outside world.

> *When humans participate in ceremony, they enter a sacred space.... All is made new; everything becomes sacred.*
>
> —SUN BEAR

This sanctuary of the heart is the secret garden where you go to retreat and to commune with God and with your own inner teacher, your Higher Self. Think of it as your private meditation room. Here you can tell God how much you love him. You can send God your intense gratitude for the blessings you have received. Then invite the angels and masters into your life to help you achieve your spiritual and material goals for the day.

Two key principles to keep in mind are that

spoken prayer is more effective than silent prayer* and we can enhance our prayer force when we are specific in naming our goals and visualizing what we want to take place.

In your prayers, name the exact conditions you want the angels to take care of in your personal life, your community and the world, such as crime, corruption, poverty, child abuse, economic problems, pollution. The more specific your prayers are, the more specific the results will be. You can offer prayers like these:

> O God, *connect with me now as I go forth this day to fulfill my highest calling. Protect my soul. Protect my time. Protect my harmony. See that I take up the cause of my service to life unperturbed. I call for divine intercession from you and your angels, and I accept it done this hour in full power.*
>
> *Angels of light, remove all obstacles to the service I am to perform for God this day. Take command of the meeting*

---

*See pages 53–58.

I will be attending with [name participants] *at* [location and time] *and lead us to the best possible outcome!*

Beloved inner Christ, beloved inner Buddha, teach me how to be more loving and compassionate today and help me not to become angry or frustrated. Direct me to the right place at the right time to find the job I need!

Beloved angels, go forth today and each day to protect my children and every child and teenager throughout the world. Protect them from every form of danger to their bodies, minds and souls. Raise up their parents and teachers, and bring into their lives the role models and guidance they need to fulfill their unique life plan.

Let all my prayers be adjusted to God's will.

Whenever you offer a prayer, it is received instantaneously by God and his angels, whose job it is to implement your requests, as long as they are in line with God's will. Because we may not know what is the highest good in a given situation, we should always ask God to adjust our prayers according to whatever is best for our soul or those for whom we are praying. Our prayers are *always* answered—but not always in the way we expect. Sometimes there is a lesson we must learn or there is another solution to the problem we just don't see.

When you pray for yourself or someone in need, you can also maximize your prayer by including all those with a like need. For instance, when praying for a friend with AIDS, you can also pray for "all those who are suffering from AIDS or any other life-threatening disease."

Whatever prayers and meditations you give during your morning ritual, it's a good idea to begin by calling for spiritual protection for yourself and your loved ones. I recommend two simple prayers for protection—the "Tube of Light" and "Traveling Protection."

As you give the "Tube of Light" affirmation,

a cylinder of white light will descend from Spirit in answer to your call. The saints and mystics of the world's religions have seen this white light in their meditations and prayers. The Israelites experienced the tube of light as a "pillar of a cloud" by day and "a pillar of fire" by night as they journeyed through the wilderness. And God promised through the prophet Zechariah: "I will be unto her [Jerusalem] a wall of fire around about, and will be the glory in the midst."

The white light can help you stay centered and at peace. It guards you from negative energies that may be directed at you through someone's anger, condemnation, hatred or jealousy. When you are unprotected, those aggressive energies can make you irritable or depressed. They can even cause you to have accidents.

The white light can also protect you from the pull of the mass consciousness. When we feel exhausted after a trip into the city or after we go shopping at a mall, it's often because our physical *and* spiritual reserves have literally been drained.

It's best to give the "Tube of Light" affirmation each morning before the hustle and bustle of the day begins. If throughout the day you feel de-energized, depleted or vulnerable, withdraw for a few minutes and repeat this prayer.

To enhance your morning ritual of protection, you can also give "Traveling Protection" or other prayers to Archangel Michael. He is the most revered of angels in several of the world's religious traditions, including Judaism, Christianity and Islam. In one of the Dead Sea Scrolls, Michael is the "mighty, ministering angel" through whom God promises to "send perpetual help" to the sons of light. In the early Christian community, Archangel Michael was a heavenly healer and protector. Called Mika'il in Muslim lore, he is the angel of nature who provides both food and knowledge to man.

> *Prayer should be the key of the day and the lock of the night.*
>
> —THOMAS FULLER

As you experiment with the techniques on the

following pages, remember that visualization can enhance the benefits of your prayers. That's because whatever you put your attention on, you are "plugging into" and charging with energy. The image we hold in our mind's eye is like a blueprint, and our attention is the magnet that attracts the creative energies of Spirit to fill it in. "We are what we think," taught Gautama Buddha, "having become what we thought."

Therefore when you pray, you can visualize the exact outcome you are praying for as if it were already taking place in the present. See it as if it were happening on a movie screen in front of you. If you don't have a specific outcome in mind, then concentrate on the words of the prayer and see the action they describe taking place before you.

Spiritual Exercises

■ **Create a personal altar.** Find a place in your home where you can set up your personal sacred space and altar, even if it's a corner of your bedroom or living room (as described on pages 39–40).

■ **Be specific.** Take time to write down your divine "wish list." Don't hold back or limit what you think God can do. Expect miracles!

Then, as part of your morning ritual of spiritual connection and prayer, be *creative* and *specific* in formulating your calls for divine action. Name aloud the specific activities and outcomes you want to see take place that day, the conditions you want redressed, the situations you want resolved.

Don't forget to name those who need God's healing light and to visualize the outcomes you want to see take place.

■ **Begin each day by establishing a protective light** around yourself and loved ones by giving the "Tube of Light" affirmation three times.

Visualization:

As you recite this affirmation, see yourself as depicted in the Chart of Your Divine Self (page 80). Your Higher Self is above you. Above your Higher Self is your I AM Presence, the presence of God with you.

See and feel a waterfall of dazzling white light, brighter than the sun shining on new-fallen snow, tumbling down from your I AM Presence to envelop you. See it coalescing to form an impenetrable wall of light.

Inside that scintillating aura of white light, see yourself surrounded with the violet flame of the Holy Spirit, a powerful high-frequency spiritual energy that transforms negativity (your own or another's) into positive and loving energy.*

From time to time throughout the day, reinforce this spiritual protection by repeating the prayer and visualizing yourself enfolded by the tube of light.

*See pages 98–103.

Tube of Light

Beloved I AM Presence bright,
Round me seal your tube of light
From ascended master flame
Called forth now in God's own name.
Let it keep my temple free
From all discord sent to me.

I AM calling forth violet fire
To blaze and transmute all desire,
Keeping on in freedom's name
Till I AM one with the violet flame.

■ **Fortify yourself with calls to Archangel Michael** for spiritual strength and protection. Give the following "Traveling Protection" prayer three times or as many times as you wish. If you don't have time to say this prayer in the morning (either at your altar or while you're getting ready for the day), you can recite it aloud as you drive to work,[10] give it quietly as you walk to your destination, or say it silently as you ride the bus or subway.

Visualization:

Visualize Archangel Michael as a majestic angel, arrayed in shining armor and wearing a cape of brilliant sapphire blue (the color of protection). See him placing his magnificent presence around you, your family, your friends and all those for whom you are praying.

Traveling Protection

Lord* Michael before,
Lord Michael behind,
Lord Michael to the right,
Lord Michael to the left,
Lord Michael above,
Lord Michael below,
Lord Michael, Lord Michael
wherever I go!

I AM his love protecting here!
I AM his love protecting here!
I AM his love protecting here!

---

* *Lord* is used in this prayer as a term of honor, denoting that Archangel Michael carries the power and presence of God.

The Creative Power of Sound

Scientific advances and studies are pointing to what healers and sages knew thousands of years ago: sound is a key to physical, emotional and spiritual vitality. Today ultrasound (high-pitched sound waves) is being used for everything from cleaning wounds to diagnosing tumors to pulverizing kidney stones. Someday it may even be used to inject drugs into the body, making needles obsolete.

Alternative health practitioners are experimenting with using specific tones to heal the organs. And certain kinds of classical music, by composers like Bach, Mozart and Beethoven, have been shown to accelerate learning, temporarily raise IQ and expand memory.

The creative power of sound is also at the heart of the world's spiritual traditions, East and West, whether as the Jewish Shema and Amidah, the Christian Our Father, the

Muslim Shahadah, the Hindu Gayatri or the Buddhist Om Mani Padme Hum.

Hindu writings contain powerful accounts of yogis who have used mantras for protection and wisdom, to enhance their concentration and meditation, and to help them achieve enlightenment and oneness with God. In Jewish mystical tradition, Kabbalists teach that by calling upon and meditating on the names of God, we can tap into an infinite source of power to restore peace and harmony to this world. Catholic tradition tells us that Saint Clare of Assisi saved her convent during an attack by Saracens when she held up the Eucharist and prayed aloud.

The greatest revolutionaries—revolutionaries of the spirit—saw prayer, especially spoken prayer, as one of the chief instruments of change. How many times have we turned on the TV set and looked on in dismay at the helpless children caught in the latest episode of ethnic cleansing? Or watched the victims of an earthquake or tornado digging through the rubble that used to be their home? How many times have we wondered how we could help? The creative power of sound gives us a way to do just that.

The prayers and affirmations included in this book are meant to be given aloud as a dynamic prayer form known as "decrees." Decrees, like other prayers, are spoken petitions to God. When we meditate, we commune with God. When we pray, we communicate with God and request his help. When we decree, we are communing, communicating and directing God's light into our world to change the circumstances we see around us. We are, in effect, commanding the flow of energy from Spirit to matter.

This is what God asked us to do when he said through the prophet Isaiah, "Ask me of things to come concerning my sons, and concerning the work of my hands *command ye me*," and when he said to Job, "Thou shalt make thy prayer unto him [the Almighty], and he shall hear thee.... Thou shalt also *decree a thing,* and it shall be established unto thee."[11] When you use the creative power of sound through spoken prayers or decrees, you are not just "asking" for help; you are entering into a partnership and an interactive relationship with God.

Prayer, meditation and decrees are all ways of plugging into the divine, and there is a time and place to practice each type of devotion. Decrees combine prayer, meditation, affirmation and visualization, and devotees from many spiritual traditions have found that this accelerated prayer form greatly enhances their own spiritual practice.

> *Properly understood and applied, [prayer] is the most potent instrument of action.*
>
> —MOHANDAS GANDHI

Decrees, like prayers and mantras, are meant to be repeated, just as Catholics repeat the Hail Mary and Buddhists their sacred chants. People often wonder why we should have to ask God for something more than once. Repeating a prayer or decree is not simply making a request over and over. It is an energy equation. Each time you repeat it, you are building a momentum. You are invoking more and more spiritual light into the situation to bring greater assistance to meet that need.

Both mystics and scientists have demonstrated the benefits of repetitive prayer. Over the centuries, mystics of the Eastern Orthodox Church reported extraordinary mystical experiences through their tradition of repeating the simple prayer: "Lord Jesus Christ, have mercy on me."

Dr. Herbert Benson, president and founder of the Mind/Body Medical Institute at Harvard Medical School, found that those who repeated Sanskrit mantras for as little as ten minutes a day experienced physiological changes—reduced heart rate, lower stress levels and slower metabolism. Subsequent studies showed that repeating mantras can benefit the immune system, relieve insomnia, reduce visits to the doctor and even increase self-esteem. When Benson and his colleagues tested other prayers, including "Lord Jesus Christ, have mercy on me," they found that they had the same positive effect. In short, repetitive prayer energizes.

Decrees are normally given three times or in multiples of three. When we give a decree three times, it keys into the power of the Trinity. It also creates a multiplication factor so that the decree has the added impetus of the "three-times-three," or the power of nine.

The prayers and decrees throughout this book are taken from the words of the saints and masters of East and West. Because these enlightened ones have reached the highest levels of intimate communion with God, their words are like ropes that we too can use to sustain a strong spiritual connection. They are sacred formulas for the release of God's power.

Call the angels into action in your life

No longer do I want you to converse with men, but with angels.

—JESUS TO SAINT TERESA OF AVILA

The word *angel* is derived from the Greek word *angelos,* meaning "messenger." The angels are indeed heralds—as well as helpers and healers, teachers and friends. I like to think of angels as extensions of the presence of God, created to be "angles" of God's consciousness. They represent and amplify the divine attributes and they give us the very personal support we need for our sojourn on earth.

Saint Basil said, "It is a teaching of Moses

that every believer has an angel to guide him as a teacher and a shepherd." The early church fathers held that every city, town and village—even every parish and family—has a special guardian angel. The Hebrews and some early Christians taught that even nations have their own guardian angels.

Islamic tradition says there are four guardian angels assigned to protect each of us, two during the day and two at night. (They must be working on round-the-clock shifts!) Other angels are described as "pious travelers," who scan the country and report back to Allah all that they observe. In Zoroastrian tradition, the Amesha Spentas, comparable to the Judeo-Christian archangels or Kabbalah's sefirot, personify divine attributes and work to defeat evil and promote good.

Some people say, "If there are all these angels waiting to help us, then why haven't they already done something about this problem in my life or in my neighborhood?" But what they don't realize is that the universe doesn't work in a top-down management style; it's based on free will and team work.

When God created us, he gave us free will so we could exercise our individuality. God doesn't go back on his word. He respects our free will. You can think of earth as a laboratory where God has given us the freedom to experiment and evolve. If, like an indulgent and overbearing parent, God sent his angels to rush in and stop us every time we were about to make a mistake, we wouldn't experience the results of our good and bad choices—which is how we learn our lessons and grow spiritually.

So, according to universal law, we need to ask God and the angels to intervene in our affairs. When we do ask, we are giving them the power to act on our behalf and do what's best for us. We are entering into a partnership with the divine, a union of heaven and earth—team work.

I have received many letters over the years telling me how angels saved the day. Someone once wrote and told me that he was returning home with friends from a seminar when he ran into some car problems. "When I was driving home," he said, "my car developed a problem and began to seriously overheat. None of us had any money to spare and were going home 'on a wing and a prayer'—literally.

"Each time the needle started creeping up hotter and hotter, I would make fiery calls to the angels. I told the people in the car to hold the visualization of snow, of crystal clear, cold mountain streams and ice all around the whole engine. Then we would watch the needle immediately go right back down as the temperature dropped to normal. It was such a wonderful testimony to the power of the spoken word and the intercession of heavenly helpers."

> *If these beings guard you, they do so because they have been summoned by your prayers.*
>
> —SAINT AMBROSE

At times we may not be aware of an impending danger, yet without asking for their intercession the angels work overtime to warn and protect us. This is especially true if we have established an ongoing relationship with the angels and we have a momentum on inviting them into our lives. The angels can also come to our aid if someone has been praying on our behalf or if we have earned a special protection in return for something good we have done in the past.

That was no doubt the case in this incident a woman related to me. One night she suddenly awoke with her hand wrapped around her breast, her fingers grasping what turned out to be a four-inch tumor. "I felt an angelic presence next to me at my bedside," she wrote. " 'Wake up! We have work to do!' was the message. I was instantly awake, every cell of my body alert. My first thought was, 'This is not going to be fun. It's cancer and it's going to be hard.' It was true. It *was* cancer and it *was* hard."

From time to time along the way, she again felt that angelic vibration that had awakened her in the middle of the night. "It seemed to be leading me onward," she said. For example, the day before she was to have surgery, she was scheduled to go to a doctor's appointment. She had been sleeping only two or three hours at night and was not digesting her food. "Do I have the strength to go to this appointment?" she thought as she lay in bed. That was when she saw the angels enter the room.

"As many as twenty came toward me," she wrote. "It seemed that I was raised up off the bed about eight inches as they approached. The angels ministered to me, lined up on both sides, ever so gently moving their hands in waves over my body. I felt great love flowing to me. As they withdrew, it seemed that I was lowered back to the bed.

"As I roused myself to go to the appointment, I realized I was strong and light as a feather. The angels had come to strengthen me. I negotiated my interview with the oncologist with finesse and sailed through the surgery the next day."

Especially touching are the accounts of angelic assistance to children, like this one describing an unforgettable intervention that had taken place years before. "I was about ten or eleven years old," the letter began. "It was a hot summer day. My father had just picked up my sister and me from our summer camp and we were driving home. I was exhausted and sleepy—so sleepy that I thought it would be wonderful to lean my head up against the car door and fall asleep. As I was about to do this, a strange yet beautiful thing happened.

"I heard a voice. I shall never forget that voice. It was a female voice—firm yet gentle, commanding yet soothing. The voice spoke to me and said (if I may paraphrase), 'No, do not lay down your head. Wait until you get home.'

"I do not have the words to describe the beauty of this voice or the depth of this being's care for me. I instantly obeyed her command and raised myself to a more upright position. Shortly thereafter—seconds or minutes—our car was hit broadside by another car. The side on which I was sitting was completely smashed in.

"If I had laid my head down as I had

intended, I may have incurred severe head injuries and perhaps died. The angels are such amazing helpers."

Fortunately, we don't have to wait for miracles like this to happen. The more we learn about how to work with angels, the more they can help us create miracles—every day. There is no problem too big or too small to assign to the angels, whether it's retrieving something you've lost, giving you strength to let go of old hurts, helping you find a new job, or even stopping war.

Although we tend to think that all angels look and act alike, Origen of Alexandria taught that all beings are assigned respective offices and duties based on their previous actions and merits. Even the archangels and their angelic assistants specialize in certain jobs, and we can call upon different bands of angels to help us in the various areas of our lives.[12]

This doesn't have to take long. Whenever you are feeling burdened or are faced with a problem, you can offer quick spoken prayers to bring the angels right into your home or your workplace or wherever you are at that moment. God wants us to take command of our world and use our free will to forge a divine partnership with Spirit. That's one of the reasons we're here on earth.

How long does it really take to direct the angels into a situation of need by naming the specific conditions we want them to tackle? About thirty seconds. How different the world would be if at the top of

Make yourself familiar with the angels… for, without being seen, they are present with you.

—SAINT FRANCIS DE SALES

each hour we would all take just thirty seconds to compose a quick prayer and send the angels on their way! When you're watching the news, you can even turn down the volume during commercials and give your calls to the angels.

As one young woman told me, "By using the science of the spoken word, I can do something for the good of the world wherever

I am—at home, in a car or hiking in the mountains. I can make the minutes of my life count for something as I invoke protection and assistance for those in need."

Remember, when you say these spoken prayers, don't be meek. You can give these calls as dynamic commands. The greater your fervor, the greater will be the response from heaven.

How many days do you have to concentrate on a specific prayer before you see results? It depends on how severe the situation is and how much of God's light is needed to displace the darkness.

For years a dear friend of mine used to rise every single morning to give prayers and decrees on behalf of the youth of the world. And she would still be doing it today if she were here among us. On the other hand, sometimes one fervent, heartfelt call can turn things around.

NAME OF ARCHANGEL	AREA OF EXPERTISE
Michael	*protection, power, faith, goodwill*
Jophiel	*wisdom, understanding, enlightenment*
Chamuel	*love, compassion, kindness, charity*
Gabriel	*purity, discipline, joy*
Raphael	*truth, science, healing, abundance, vision, music*
Uriel	*service, ministration, peace, brotherhood*
Zadkiel	*mercy, forgiveness, justice, freedom, transmutation*

Spiritual Exercises

■ **Create your own miracles every day by working with the angels.** First, write down a situation you or someone else needs help with.

Each of the seven archangels and their bands have a field of expertise, so to speak. From the chart on the previous page, choose the archangel you want to work with, the one who specializes in your area of concern.

Every day (whenever you have a moment between tasks or a break in the day) give aloud a heartfelt prayer to this archangel. Be specific and creative in your prayer, naming the exact problem and the outcome you want to see.

Here is an example of the kind of prayer you can give:

> *Archangel* [insert name of archangel] *and your bands of angels, move into action now to take command of* [name the exact situation, location and outcome you want to see].
>
> *I ask you to bring about the best and highest outcome and to multiply my prayers for the blessing of all souls in a similar predicament.*

As you say your prayer, turn the problem over to the angels. Visualize the resolution of the problem taking place before your eyes—you land the perfect job, a rocky relationship is mended, the crime rate in your neighborhood goes down.

■ **Enlist the aid of Archangel Michael**—anytime, anywhere. Here's an example of a quick and powerful SOS you can give to bring Archangel Michael to the scene:

> *Archangel Michael,*
> *help me, help me, help me!*
> *Archangel Michael,*
> *help me, help me, help me!*
> *Archangel Michael,*
> *help me, help me, help me!*

As you repeat these words, send an arc of light from your heart to the heart of this magnificent archangel. When you make that call with fervor, Archangel Michael will instantaneously be at your side.

Here is another simple decree to Archangel Michael you can give:

> O dearest Michael, archangel of faith,
> Around my life protection seal;
> Let each new day my faith increase
> That God in life is all that's real.
>
> Go before me, Michael dear,
> Thy shield of faith I do revere;
> Armor of light's living flame,
> Manifest action in God's name.

(See also "Traveling Protection" to Archangel Michael on page 52.)

Let your spiritual self do the work

I have seen that in any great undertaking
it is not enough for a man to depend
simply upon himself.

—ISNA-LA-WICA (LONE MAN)

The ancient Chinese sage Lao Tzu taught, "Act without doing. Work without effort."

To the Western mind, this sounds like a Zen koan. How can you act without *doing,* or work without *effort*?

Lao Tzu was revealing the secret that all spiritual adepts have discovered. He was telling us that when our lesser self (our ego) gets out of the way, then our greater self (our spiritual self) can act through us effortlessly. Lao Tzu put it another way when he said, "To become full, be empty.... He who knows...humility becomes the valley of the world." In other words, he who has humbled the ego creates the sacred space that can cradle Spirit.

> *[The sage] never strives himself for the great, and thereby the great is achieved.*
>
> —LAO TZU

In Taoist terms, when we are "empty" we can be filled with the Tao—the all-pervading Spirit, the Ultimate Reality. To put it in modern parlance: we can't be full of ourselves and full of the Spirit at the same time.

We have a spiritual self that is our true nature. The lower self, the human ego, eclipses the sun of that spiritual self and gets in the way. We can integrate more spirituality into our lives when we become empty and open, like a valley, and consciously allow our spiritual self to teach us and to express through us.

The nineteenth-century Hindu saint Rama-krishna expressed it this way: "I am the machine, Thou [God, the Higher Self] art the operator.... I speak as Thou makest me speak. I act as Thou makest me act."[13] Jesus was telling us the same truth when he taught, "I can of mine own self do nothing.... The Father that dwelleth in me, he doeth the work." The Hasidic teacher Dov Baer summed it up when he said, "Whatever one does, God is doing it."

If we can let go of the ego's need to control, if we can hand over the situation to God, to our spiritual self, we open the door to possibilities we never thought of before. "It is the sense of struggle that makes the struggle," says the ascended master Saint Germain.

Sometimes our overconcern or anxiety are like blinders. When we have blinders on, we have a very narrow view and we can't possibly see all the options. In fact, we may be looking for answers in all the wrong places. When we're open to another way of seeing things—when we can relax, move into a receptive mode and open up like a valley—then the God within can bring the highest solution to us.

My late husband and teacher, Mark L. Prophet, used to say we are never going to find the answer we are looking for outside of ourselves. "It's in yourself," he said. "That's where the search begins. We can discover a gold mine of consciousness within. It is the consciousness of the indwelling Christ. And when we find that consciousness, we will have a new appreciation of our net worth. You don't find your net worth on a financial statement; you find it inside of you."

God is no botcher.

—JOHN HEYWOOD

Spiritual Exercises ─────────────────────────

■ **Take a step back.** Letting your spiritual self do the work is an attitude, a way of life. If something in your life seems too hard to do, take a step back, consciously turn over the problem to your Higher Self and let go. Say a prayer surrendering the problem, even a simple prayer like one of the following or the longer "Prayer for Attunement" on the next page.

God, you take command of this situation. I just can't do it myself. But I know you can do it.

Beloved Christ Self, enter into the vacuum of my being and act through me this day for the highest good in this situation. Cut me free from all self-limitation, spiritual blindness and unhealthy habits that do not enable me to see thee and thy will clearly, O God.

Prayer for Attunement

Beloved mighty I AM Presence,
  act on my behalf this day:
Fill my form.
Release the light that is necessary
  for me to go forth to do thy will,
And see that at every hand the decisions I make
  are according to thy holy will.
See that my energies are used to magnify
  the Lord in everyone whom I meet.
See to it that thy holy wisdom released to me
  is used constructively for the expansion
  of God's kingdom.
And above all, beloved heavenly Father,
  I commend my spirit unto thee.
And I ask that as thy flame is one with my flame,
  the union of these two flames shall pulsate
  to effect in my world the continuous
  alertness and attunement which I need
  with thy holy Presence, with the Holy Spirit
  and with the World Mother.

Your Spiritual Anatomy

Each of us has a unique spiritual self with a vast spiritual potential. We have a personal connection with God right inside of us. The Chart of Your Divine Self, depicted on page 80, can help us understand this relationship.

This illustration is a portrait of you and of the God within you. It is a diagram of your spiritual anatomy and your potential to become who you really are. Author Dannion Brinkley, who has had three near-death experiences, says, "This is what you look like from spiritual realms."

The upper figure in the Chart of Your Divine Self is the I AM Presence, the Presence of God that is individualized in each one of us. Buddhists call it the Dharmakaya, the body of Ultimate Reality. Your I AM Presence is your personalized "I AM THAT I AM," the name of God that was revealed to Moses. "I AM THAT I AM" means simply but profoundly

As above, so below. As God is in heaven, so God is on earth within me. Right where I stand, God is. I am here on earth the "I AM" that is in Spirit.

In spiritual dimensions, your I AM Presence is surrounded by seven concentric spheres of spiritual energy that make up what is called the causal body. These spheres of pulsating energy contain the record of the good works you have performed.

The middle figure represents your Higher Self—your inner teacher, dearest friend and voice of conscience. Each of us is destined to embody the attributes of our Higher Self, which is sometimes referred to as the inner Christ or the inner Buddha.

The shaft of white light descending from the heart of the I AM Presence through the Higher Self to the lower figure is the crystal cord (or "silver cord," as Ecclesiastes calls it). It is the umbilical cord, or lifeline, that ties you to Spirit. Your crystal cord also nourishes the divine spark that is ensconced in the secret chamber of your heart.

The lower figure represents you on the spiritual path, surrounded by the protective white light of God and the violet flame (the purifying spiritual fire of the Holy Spirit), which you can call forth in your spiritual practices.* The purpose of your soul's evolution on earth is to grow in self-mastery, balance your karma, become one with your Higher Self, and fulfill your mission so that you can return to the spiritual dimensions that are your real home.

*See pages 51, 104–7.

Live in the present

I said there was but one solitary thing about the past worth remembering and that was the fact that it is past.

—MARK TWAIN

"Do not dwell in the past, do not dream of the future, concentrate the mind on the present moment," taught Gautama Buddha. "Renounce the craving for the past, renounce the craving for the future, renounce the craving for what is between, and cross to the opposite shore."

What is the craving for the past? It's the desire—and we all have it from time to time—

to relive the "good old days." Or it's looking back and constantly thinking about "what could have been."

What is the craving for the future? It's worrying about what *might* happen if...

What is the opposite shore? Think of it as the place you want to be—the place of peace, the place of happiness, the place where there is no more "craving."

And what is the bridge that can help us cross to that opposite shore? It's the arc of our attention.

One of the most important spiritual laws to remember is that *where your attention goes, there goes your energy.* Each day we have just so much energy allotted to us. If part of our attention is constantly fixated on the past or worrying about the future, that much less energy is available for us to use in the here and now.

It's as if the river of life flowing through us has become splintered into smaller streams. These rivulets of energy, flowing away from the main stream and the main pattern of our life, can sap us of the full power we need to carry out our life's mission. As a result we may become preoccupied, unfocused, even chronically tired or depressed.

Another factor that can keep us from concentrating fully on the present is that we may have literally left a part of ourselves somewhere else. This could be the result of a traumatic experience or abuse. Or maybe we have loved someone so much that when we lost them, a part of us remained with them. It is natural and healthy to grieve and to feel pain at the loss of a loved one. But when we don't pick up the pieces and move on, it's as if a part of our soul is missing in action.

Harboring anger or resentment or not forgiving another—*or* ourselves—also prevents us from living in the present. We think that by snubbing someone else we are cutting them out of our lives. In actuality, our anger or resentment does just the opposite; it keeps us tied to them in a karmic entanglement, and we aren't free to move on.

One of my favorite lessons on letting go of extra baggage comes from an old Buddhist story about two monks who are traveling together. They come to a stream where they meet a pretty young girl who is hesitating to cross because she doesn't want to wet her clothes. One of the monks picks her up, carries her across and continues on his way.

Monks, of course, do not normally associate with women, much less touch them, and his companion is shocked. With each step he gets more and more upset, and his preoccupation slows him down. Finally, after several miles, he can no longer contain himself and blurts out, "How could you do such a thing?"

The first monk is at first puzzled and then replies, "Oh, you mean the young girl? I put her down miles ago. Are you still carrying her?"

When we make a decision not to let go of

> *Life consists in what a man is thinking of all day.*
>
> —RALPH WALDO EMERSON

anger or an old hurt, we literally carry it around with us. I have learned that being angry or resentful is a vicious circle. It drains us of our energy because part of us is always focused on that unresolved situation. When we forgive, we free up 100 percent of our energy for constructive endeavor.

Part of forgiving is realizing that sometimes when people wrong us it has everything to do with them and nothing to do with us. Perhaps someone's sharp words are a result of a deep inner pain that won't go away. Perhaps a frustrated friend is carrying a burden too hard to bear and her soul is crying out for help. Perhaps the "wrong" is just life's way of bringing to our attention a lesson we have refused to learn any other way. Whatever it is, we are not truly free until we resolve the anger and forgive.

There may be times when we feel we cannot forgive someone because we believe the crime he or she committed against us or a loved one has been too great. God has taught me that in a situation like this we can forgive the soul and then ask God and his angels to bind the unreal self, the dark side, of the person that caused him to commit the crime.

No matter how bad a person's deeds are, if we forgive the soul—that part of his being that still has the potential for good—we can avoid a karmic entanglement. "Hate never destroys hate," taught Gautama Buddha in those immortal words of the Dhammapada, "only love destroys hate." Hatred binds; love frees.

Sometimes the most important person you have to forgive is yourself. Whatever wrongs you have committed, you can call for forgiveness, do the spiritual and practical work of making amends, and see your mistakes as learning experiences.

"What's past is prologue" is the way Shakespeare put it. We can certainly learn from our yesterdays, but it's dangerous to live in the past. Someone once boiled it down to this: "Keep your eye on the road, and use your rearview mirror only to avoid trouble."[14]

We've talked about how living in the past

can be a trap, but the same thing goes for fixating on the future. There's nothing wrong with planning, but perpetually worrying about the future can leave us with limited energy to devote to the present. When you think about it, anxiety about the future is really doubt that our Creator, our spiritual Source, will supply us with what we need—or it's the belief that we don't deserve to receive it.

People in the West are always getting ready to live.

—CHINESE PROVERB

Nothing could be further from the truth. God has an unlimited source of energy. And it's not the universe that limits what we can receive— it's our own belief patterns. As the Taoist master Chuang Tzu taught: "The sagelike man knows the way of what the ancients called the Heavenly Treasure House.... He may pour into it without its being filled; he may pour from it without its being exhausted."

Jesus, adapting a very Eastern perspective on this, said, "Behold the fowls of the air: for

89

they sow not, neither do they reap, nor gather into barns; yet your heavenly Father feedeth them. Are ye not much better than they?... Why take ye thought for raiment? Consider the lilies of the field, how they grow; they toil not, neither do they spin.... If God so clothe the grass of the field, which today is and tomorrow is cast into the oven, shall he not much more clothe you?"[15]

May we have your comments on this book?

We hope that you have enjoyed this book and that it will occupy a special place in your library. It would be helpful to us in meeting your needs and the needs of our readers if you would fill out and mail this postage-free card to us.

Book title: _____

Your comments: _____

_____

_____

_____

_____

How did this book come to your attention? _____

How would you rate this book on a scale of 1 to 5, with 5 being the highest? _____

Topics of interest to you: _____

Would you like to receive a free catalog of our publications? ☐ Yes ☐ No

Name _____

City _____ State _____ Zip Code _____ Phone no. _____

E-mail: _____ (We will not make your name available to other companies.)

Thank you for taking the time to give us your feedback.

Call us toll free at 1-800-245-5445. Outside the U.S.A., call 406-848-9500. Summit University Press titles are available from fine bookstores everywhere. E-mail: tslinfo@tsl.org

491-APS R10/01

Spiritual Exercises —————————————————

■ **Turn it over to a higher power.** Is there something from the past or a worry about the future that preoccupies you—something you should have put down miles ago?

If you feel yourself dwelling on the past or worrying about the future, try repeating this affirmation or your own adaptation of it as well as the "Affirmations for Peace" on the following page:

> *Beloved I AM Presence,* beloved*
> [insert the name of a saint, master or angel you are
> working with], *you take command of this
> entire situation. I shall not be moved!*

---

*Your I AM Presence is the personal presence of God with you.

Affirmations for Peace

I accept the gift of peace in my heart.
I accept the gift of peace in my soul.
I accept the gift of peace in my mind
*   and in my emotions.*

I say to all that would tempt me away
*   from my center of peace:*
I shall not be moved.
Peace, be still! Peace, be still!
*   Peace, be still!*

I AM the gentle rain of peace.
I AM a servant of peace.
I AM sealed in the heart of peace.
May the world abide
*   in an aura of God's peace!*

■ **Call on the law of forgiveness.** When you have done something you later regret, call out to God and say, *"I recognize that I have hurt another part of life. I call upon the law of forgiveness from your heart, O God, for anything I may have done that was not kind, respectful, honorable, especially _____ ."*

Vow to set the record straight by making amends to those you have harmed in any way. Then offer the following affirmation as you send your love and forgiveness to all whom you have ever wronged and to all who have ever wronged you, releasing the situations into God's hands.

Decree for Forgiveness

I AM forgiveness acting here,
Casting out all doubt and fear,
Setting men forever free
With wings of cosmic victory.

I AM calling in full power
For forgiveness every hour;
To all life in every place
I flood forth forgiving grace.

8

Use spiritual energy to change your past

*If we open a quarrel between the past
and the present, we shall find
that we have lost the future.*

—WINSTON CHURCHILL

Moving beyond the past is the inner work of our soul. It is profound work, and at times hard work, because our soul knows deep within that in order to shape the future we want we also have to take accountability for the past.

Whatever we do comes full circle to our doorstep—sometime, somewhere. That's an inescapable law of the universe. In the East, it's known as the law of karma.

Karma is a Sanskrit word meaning "act," "action," "word" or "deed." Karma, both positive and negative, is the effect of causes we have set in motion in the past, whether ten minutes ago or ten embodiments ago. Karma is the consequences of our thoughts, words and deeds.

We have all grown up learning about karma. We just didn't call it that. Instead, we heard: *What goes around comes around. Whatsoever a man soweth, that shall he also reap. For every action there is an equal and opposite reaction. And in the end, the love you take is equal to the love you make...*

Every moment energy is flowing to us from God, and every moment we are deciding whether we will put a positive or negative spin on it. By the law of the circle, the law of karma, that energy will return to us. When the positive energy returns, we see positive things come into our life. The energy that has our negative stamp on it, because we have used that energy to harm rather than help others, also returns to its source—this time seeking resolution. It returns to us as opportunity to make things right.

When we don't transform that returning energy into something positive, it doesn't just go away. For example, we have free will to qualify God's energy as love or as hatred. If we have qualified it as hatred, that energy remains with us as part of our consciousness until we transmute it by love.

Negative karma can manifest as everything from ingrained habit patterns that keep us from getting along with others to disease or accidents. Groups of people can create negative "group karma" when they contribute, for instance, to pollution or persecution; and they are jointly accountable for the harm they may have caused another part of life.

Another way to understand how our past actions affect our life today is to look at the accumulation of negative karma as an energy blockage. The masters of the ancient Oriental art of Feng Shui teach that clutter in our physical environment inhibits the flow of energy (or *ch'i*) in our surroundings. They say that flow of energy (or lack of it) powerfully affects our health, our finances, our relationships—the very course of our life.

In exactly the same way, "karmic clutter" can create blockages in the flow of energy at subtle, energetic levels *within* us. These blockages affect our physical and emotional well-being, our spiritual progress, even the kinds of events and people that move in and out of our life. When energy flows freely, we feel peaceful, healthy, creative. When it is blocked, we don't feel as light, healthy, vibrant and spiritual as we could.

While we can't really change what has happened in the past, we can free ourselves and others from the burden of our past mistakes. We can do so by making amends to those we have harmed and by serving others in our community. We can also accelerate the process of clearing our karma with certain spiritual techniques.

The sacred texts of East and West tell us we can use prayers, mantras and sacred songs to purify our "sins" (negative karma), to clear the record—in effect, to change the past. As one Hindu text puts it, "The Supreme Intelligence dances in the soul... for the purpose of removing our sins. By these means, our Father scatters the darkness of illusion, burns the thread of karma, stamps down evil, showers grace." "Though your sins be as scarlet," pronounced the prophet Isaiah, "they shall be as white as snow."

In essence, the prayers and practices handed down through the world's religions are sacred formulas that call forth the light of the Holy Spirit for forgiveness and purification. In some spiritual traditions, this powerfully transforming energy of the Holy Spirit has been seen as a violet light, known as the violet flame.

Just as a ray of sunlight passing through a prism is refracted into the seven colors of the rainbow, so spiritual light manifests as seven rays, or flames. When we call forth these spiritual flames in our prayers and meditations, each flame creates a specific action in our body, mind and soul. The violet flame is the color and frequency of spiritual light that stimulates mercy, forgiveness and transmutation.

To "transmute" is to alter—to change something into a higher form. The term was used centuries ago by alchemists who attempted, on a physical level, to transmute base metals into gold —and, on a spiritual level, to achieve transformation and eternal life.

That is precisely what the violet flame can do. It is a high-frequency spiritual energy that separates out the "gross" elements of our karma from the gold of our true self so we can achieve our highest potential. It works at energetic levels to clear personal and group karma and increase the balance and flow of energy throughout our world.

> *Mankind living in the world today assume that recorded history… cannot be changed. They have not reckoned with the violet transmuting flame.*
>
> —EL MORYA

Edgar Cayce, renowned seer of the twentieth century, recognized the healing power of the violet light. In over nine hundred of his readings, he recommended an electrical device—a "violet ray" machine that emits a violet-colored electrical charge—to treat a number of ailments, including exhaustion, lethargy, poor circulation, digestive problems and nervous disorders.

Why is the violet flame such a powerful tool? In our physical world, violet light has the highest frequency in the visible spectrum. Fritjof Capra in *The Tao of Physics* explains that "violet light has a high frequency and a short wavelength and consists therefore of photons of high energy and high momentum."[16] Of all the spiritual flames, the violet flame is closest in vibratory action to the chemical elements and compounds in our physical universe, and therefore it has the greatest ability to interpenetrate and transform matter at atomic and subatomic levels.

The reason the violet flame can "change" the past, so to speak, is that at energetic levels it dissolves the record of our past actions as well as the negative karma we may have created by taking those actions. This karma, by the law of the circle, shapes our future. So if we can transmute our creations of the past, we can create a better tomorrow.

Dannion Brinkley, author of *Saved by the Light,* says that during his near-death experiences he saw and felt the violet flame. He reports that after he "died," a being of light led him to a city of crystal cathedrals, which were actually halls of learning. "Every crystal city has the violet flame as well as all the spiritual flames," he says.

> *The greatness of the violet flame is that it doesn't produce heat; it produces love.*
>
> —DANNION BRINKLEY

"But the violet flame is the greatest of the flames. The violet flame is the purest place of love. It's what really empowers you."

Dannion has also explained that the violet flame is "a light that serves all spiritual heritages, that gives respect and dignity to all things. It gives us a way to connect with each other."[17]

You can apply the violet flame to your

everyday spirituality by using the prayers and decrees given to us by the masters.[18] The violet flame lets you transmute the negatives and capitalize on the positives, and it can facilitate the healing of body, mind and soul.*

Each morning an angel brings us our karma for the day. As soon as we wake up, that package of karma is waiting for us, seeking resolution. That's why it's a good idea to give violet-flame prayers in the morning. You can recite them during your morning prayer ritual, while you're in the shower or getting ready for the day, or even as you travel to work.

Those of us who have used the violet flame in our prayers have found that it does help resolve patterns of consciousness, dispel inner pain and bring balance into our lives. It creates an awareness and an attunement with the inner self that makes for creativity and a feeling of being alive and well and in action for good on earth. It gives us a way to help mitigate condi-

---

*Please note that although the violet flame can facilitate our healing at many levels, it is not intended to replace regular medical diagnosis or to be used as a substitute for proper medical care.

tions on the world scene by clearing the real karmic cause at the core of the issues.[19]

One woman wrote to me and said, "For years I had consulted with psychologists; they had helped me to see causes, but how could I *change*?" She started working with violet-flame prayers every day and said the violet flame penetrated and dissolved core resentment. "Through the violet flame," she said, "I emerged healthy, vigorous and grateful."

Another said, "I used to think there was nothing I could do about the state of the world. I was only one person. And yet I cared deeply. The violet flame solved that problem for me. I *could* do something—and that was the spiritual work on the problems of the world. I could help tackle the problems of the environment."

I've seen thousands of people work successfully with the violet flame. It takes a different amount of time—anywhere from a day to several months—for each person to see results. But if you remain constant, you will begin to feel the difference.

Spiritual Exercises

■ **Create your own affirmations.** If you would
like to experiment with the violet flame, you can
start with this simple violet-flame affirmation,
which is meant to be repeated over and over as a
mantra that sings in your heart:

> *I AM a being of violet fire,*
> *I AM the purity God desires!*

You can also create your own variations on
the theme, wherever you perceive a need, such as:

> *My heart is alive with violet fire,*
> *My heart is the purity God desires!*

> *My family is enfolded in violet fire,*
> *My family is the purity God desires!*

> *Earth is a planet of violet fire,*
> *Earth is the purity God desires!*

■ **Energize heart, head and hand.** This next set of decrees (page 107) helps purify and energize the three major aspects of our practical spirituality—heart, head and hand.

We begin with the heart because the heart is the hub of life, physically and spiritually. The heart is the place where we commune with God. It is the center from which we send out our love to nourish mankind.

With the "Heart" mantra, we call forth the transmutative power of the violet flame to dissolve negative feelings and karma that block the flow of energy through our heart. This mantra helps us develop the qualities of the heart. It helps us become more open, more sensitive and more compassionate to the plight of so many who need our love and our prayers.

Our head is the chalice where we receive the creative thoughts of God and our Higher Self. The "Head" mantra clears the physical and spiritual faculties of the mind so that we can think and communicate more clearly. It helps us strengthen our intuitive faculties and develop a keener perception of spiritual dimensions.

Our hands represent how we put our spirituality into practice. The hand symbolizes the power of God to make things happen—through our profession, our service to life, the big and small things we do for others every day. Through our hand we can transfer tremendous energy and healing. In the "Hand" mantra we affirm that when we work hand-in-hand with God, nothing will be impossible.

Visualization:

As you recite the "Heart" mantra, visualize the violet flame within your heart as a pulsating violet light that softens your heart, transforming anger into compassion, bitterness into sweetness, anxiety into peace.

As you give the "Head" mantra, see the violet flame leaping up from your heart and penetrating into your head to clear your mind of all mental blocks, negative images and limiting concepts about yourself or others. See your mind becoming filled with the brilliant light of God.

As you give the "Hand" mantra, visualize the violet flame dissolving the cause, effect, record and memory of those things you had a "hand" in that you wish you hadn't done. You can give each section below three times, or as many times as you wish.

Heart

Violet fire, thou love divine,
Blaze within this heart of mine!
Thou art mercy forever true,
Keep me always in tune with you.

Head

I AM light, thou Christ in me,
Set my mind forever free;
Violet fire, forever shine
Deep within this mind of mine.

God who gives my daily bread,
With violet fire fill my head
Till thy radiance heavenlike
Makes my mind a mind of light.

Hand

I AM the hand of God in action,
Gaining victory every day;
My pure soul's great satisfaction
Is to walk the Middle Way.

Use every encounter and circumstance as an opportunity to grow

I learn by going where I have to go.

—THEODORE ROETHKE

Life is a mirror. People and circumstances mirror back to us the issues we need to deal with. When we are in a difficult or unpleasant situation, our knee-jerk reaction is often to kick and fuss, run in the opposite direction, or just shut down so we don't have to deal with it. There's another alternative: fully enter into the situation in order to learn from it.

The reason this alternative is so effective is that it accelerates the inevitable process of resolution. While we may be able to run away from a situation, the issues that underlie it won't disappear. They follow us around like the hound of heaven, perhaps under other guises, until we deal with them. Without that hound of heaven we wouldn't grow spiritually or balance our karma.

There are no coincidences in the universe. Whoever comes knocking at your door (or bursting into your office) is bringing a message. And, believe it or not, our souls have sometimes been waiting a long, long time for those messengers to appear.

This old Tibetan tale is full of meaning for our own lives. One day a venerable Buddhist monk was in the forest bending over a large pot in which he was dyeing his ocher-colored robe. A group of men looking for a missing baby cow stumbled upon the monk. When they saw that what was in his pot was blood-colored, they accused him of stealing and killing the cow, and they dragged him in front of a kangaroo court in the neighboring village. Then they chained him and put him in a hole in the ground. Yet the monk did not say a word to defend himself—to the chagrin of his disciples, who knew he was a vegetarian and would never have stolen the cow.

A few days later, the villagers found the baby cow and asked the local chieftain to release the monk. The chieftain, however, got caught up in timely matters and the monk remained in the pit for months. At last one of his disciples obtained an audience with the king and told him what had happened. Afraid that misfortune would befall his kingdom because of the mistake, he ordered the monk to be released immediately and begged his forgiveness, promising to punish those who were responsible.

The monk, however, implored the king to punish no one. "It was my turn to suffer," he admitted.

"How could that be?" asked the surprised sovereign.

The monk explained that in a past life he had stolen a baby cow. While escaping from his pursuers, he had abandoned it near a holy man meditating in the forest. The holy man was blamed for the crime and chained in a hole for

six days. "I have been waiting lifetimes to ex-
piate my sin, and I am grateful to your subjects
for bringing me the opportunity to be free of
this karma," said the monk. Having finished
his story, he retreated into the forest to once
again take up his spiritual practices.[20]

Many of the circumstances of our lives are
just like that. Life is a
great teacher. As psycho-
analyst Karen Horney
once commented, "For-
tunately [psycho]analy-
sis is not the only way to
resolve inner conflicts. Life itself remains a very
effective therapist." Often we keep attracting to
ourselves the same kinds of people and the same
kinds of situations until we embrace the opportunity to balance the karma and learn our lesson.

*If the messenger
be an ant, heed him.*

— EL MORYA

If you have unresolved issues with your
father or mother, for example, you'll keep attracting to yourself relationships and people
who force those same issues into the foreground.
If we tend to be judgmental, we'll probably keep

111

bumping into people who incite our criticism until we learn to love everyone—and until we find out why we have the *need* to be critical. For the old adage is true: We can't really change another; we can only change ourselves. We can't necessarily change what happens to us; we can only change our reaction to it.

Life is a lot like the movie *Groundhog Day*. We have to keep playing out the same scenes over and over and over again until we finally get it right. Everything is a lesson designed to help us gain self-mastery so we can pass our exams and graduate from earth's schoolroom.

Sometimes the events that happen to us, though they seem catastrophic, are what push us out of our box to explore new vistas. The renowned twentieth-century illustrator Norman Rockwell came face-to-face with this initiation when, after completing his monumental works portraying the Four Freedoms, his studio caught fire and burned to the ground. He lost everything—his antiques and artwork, his costumes and clippings, his paints and his beloved pipes.

Twenty-eight years of painting, traveling and collecting were destroyed.

Rockwell treated the fire with humor publicly. He even published a funny sketch in the *Saturday Evening Post* depicting the details of the incident. But it must have been a devastating experience. In his autobiography, in a chapter entitled "I Rise from the Ashes," he wrote, "It's just like losing your left arm, and waking up in the middle of the night and reaching out for a glass of water and suddenly realizing that you haven't got anything to reach with."[21]

The event marked a kind of turning point for the artist. He decided that all along he had really wanted to move to a less secluded home. He found one and began to build a new studio. Some observers say that without his old props to rely on, his work changed too. More than ever, he took his artistry on location to portray the world around him. The trial by fire brought Rockwell to another level and triggered his next leap in soul growth.

Spiritual Exercises

■   **Ask the obvious.** The next time you find yourself in a situation you'd rather avoid, ask yourself: *What can I learn from this encounter? What message is God sending me? Rather than running away, what can I do to bring resolution?*

■   **Look for the patterns and ask yourself:** *What circumstances or kinds of people keep moving into my life as a repetitive pattern?* (For example, do you keep getting jobs where your manager or co-workers make you feel _____, or do you find yourself in friendships or relationships where your friends or partners make you feel _____?)

What positive behavior do I want to develop so I can break free of those patterns? (For example, to bring about soul growth do you need to give support to your managers rather than criticize—or be honest and stand up for yourself? Do you need to open your heart—or draw healthy boundaries?)

Practice loving-kindness toward everyone— including yourself

One kind word can warm
three winter months.

—JAPANESE PROVERB

When a child is learning to write his letters and he shows you his first crude attempt, you tell him what a wonderful job he has done. You don't belittle him because the curves of his *s* are going the wrong way. You praise him, and the little smile he flashes your way is your reward.

What if we did that with everyone we met? What if we decided not to dwell on another's imperfections but to love and support the soul who is striving to become whole? What if we treated each person the same way we would treat the little child who just showed us his first picture of daddy or his first attempt to write the alphabet?

When we send others a positive signal of how wonderful they are, even if they aren't exhibiting it in that moment, we are supporting them while they grow into that matrix. If, on the other hand, we criticize, condemn or gossip about them, we reinforce the momentums of their lesser self rather than accentuate the positives of their spiritual self.

I have found that the best byword is not to say anything about anybody that you wouldn't say to his or her face. And for every person you meet, find the nicest thing you can say about him that's true. Then say it. If you have to give feedback, try to do it in a way that is helpful and not harmful, constructive and not condemning.

There is a wonderful Hasidic tale that teaches this lesson. A highly revered rabbi made it a habit of inviting his friends and students to share his table at the Sabbath meal. On one of these occasions an uncouth, sloppily dressed man entered the room and took a seat. The rabbi's students looked down their noses at him as he proceeded to pull out of his pocket a large radish.

The rabbi seemed oblivious to the loud crunching that was emitting from the other end of the table. Finally one of the students, trying not to let the rabbi hear him, asked the visitor how he had the nerve to disturb the decorum of their most revered host's repast. Just then the rabbi casually remarked, "It would be wonderful if I had a really good radish to eat right now."

The radish eater, with a big smile on his face, produced from his pocket another big, tangy, red root. The rabbi praised his guest for his generosity and then munched on the radish with delight.[22]

The rabbi understood that criticizing his guest wasn't going to do any good—and, in fact, there wasn't anything to criticize him for.

Instead the rabbi searched for the one thing that would lift the man's self-esteem in that moment. That is one of the most beautiful gifts we can give to others—*helping them recognize in themselves what is so special about them.*

> *That best portion of a good man's life,— his little, nameless, unremembered acts of kindness.*
>
> —WILLIAM WORDSWORTH

When we talk about loving-kindness, there is one person we absolutely cannot leave out of the picture—ourselves. Gautama Buddha once said, "You can look the whole world over and never find anyone more deserving of love than yourself."

This is such a hard concept for many of us to accept. But if you think about your origins, your divine origins, it's not hard to accept at all. You are a son or daughter of God, and God loves you just as a father and mother love their child. So if you condemn yourself, you are actually condemning a part of God. Think about that the next time you get down on yourself—or anyone else.

We all make mistakes, but it's dangerous to tell yourself, "Well, because I did such and such I'm just not good enough for God or even the smallest angel to pay any attention to today."

It's good to feel that you are doing something that would please God, but remember that God loves you first and foremost *for who you are,* not for what you do. It's a sweet and tender moment when you realize that it's not because you have accomplished something that God loves you; God loves you because *you are who you are.*

When we do fall short of the mark, God doesn't take out a whip. God says, "Pick yourself up. Brush off the dust. Be sure you learn a lesson. Next time you'll conquer, because you will have recognized the dangers and pitfalls of that particular path."

Self-condemnation is one of the biggest challenges on the spiritual path. It can severely stunt our spiritual growth, and we're the only ones who can really do something about it. "No one," said Eleanor Roosevelt, "can make you feel inferior without your consent."

If we don't press beyond the limitations that we or others impose upon us, we will always hit a ceiling—a ceiling we have created because we have convinced ourselves that we are not capable of going any higher and don't deserve to.

If we have a deep belief that we can't succeed or we don't deserve to have a good relationship or a good job, then we will sabotage ourselves. Sadly, some people fail at whatever they are doing just to prove to themselves and everyone else that they are just not good enough. It's a subconscious mechanism—failing as a means of inflicting self-punishment, failing in order to prove to everyone that they are as bad as they (or others) affirm that they are.

The breakthrough can only come when we look to the spiritual part of ourselves, not the human part. People believe they or others aren't good enough because they look at the human part of the personality—the foibles and idiosyncrasies we are all heir to—and they become disappointed. But we aren't perfecting the human part of ourselves. We are maturing the spiritual part of ourselves. That's what really counts.

Spiritual Exercises ─────────────────

■ **Use sign language.** If you have a problem with self-esteem, try making a sign that says: *"God loves me because I am who I am."* Then tack up that sign on your bathroom mirror or somewhere where you will see it every day.

■ **Truthfully appreciate others.** To generate loving-kindness, when you see someone coming toward you, take a mental snapshot. By the time she has reached you, think of the most loving thing you can say to her in that moment, and make sure that you're being truthful.

■ **Start an appreciation journal or folder.** When someone tells you something wonderful about yourself—something that is an expression of your higher nature—write it down. And thank God for endowing you with that special gift and giving you the opportunity to share it with another.

We don't always notice or remember when

the gold of our true self is shining through. Writing down these precious observations can help us be kind to ourselves in those moments when we get discouraged.

A Prayer for the Balm of Gilead

O love of God, immortal love,
   Enfold all in thy ray;
Send compassion from above
   To raise them all today!
In the fullness of thy power,
   Shed thy glorious beams
Upon the earth and all thereon
   Where life in shadow seems!
Let the light of God blaze forth
   To cut men free from pain;
Raise them up and clothe them, God,
   With thy mighty I AM name!

11

Take time for physical and spiritual renewal

If they ask you, "What is the sign of
your father in you?" say to them,
"It is movement and repose."

—THE GOSPEL OF THOMAS

Creative tension is what produces the dynamic movement that is life. In Chinese philosophy, the interplay of the two basic components of the universe, the yin and yang of the T'ai Chi, creates all change in the universe. These two forces—the masculine and feminine, the positive and negative—oppose yet complement each other. They are in constant flux.

Just think about the experiences you have

had where you were propelled to a new level—whether it was taking your first steps, learning how to ride a bike, or mastering a new sport or skill. Didn't this breakthrough always involve creative tension—a stretching of the sinews? Creative tension brings out the best in us. It impels us to come up higher. Without it, we wouldn't give birth to a new and higher part of ourselves.

Creative tension involves pulling back the arrow and having a taut string so that the arrow can fly fast and far. There is, however, an ebb and flow in the process. When the arrow is shot from the bow, there is a point of release and relaxation. At that point of release, we regroup and prepare for the next challenge.

The healthy way to live with creative tension is to take advantage of the naturally occurring cycles of physical and spiritual renewal. Even in an intense cycle, don't forget to allow yourself time for renewal. Take fifteen minutes to do something that replenishes you. If we don't learn to do this, our body will force us to.

A friend of mine once told me she was

working with someone who had had surgery some months earlier. When my friend asked her how she was feeling, the woman joked, "Well, if I don't get some time off soon, I'm going to start planning my next surgery." Unfortunately, that's no joke. If we don't pay attention to our need for renewal—physical and spiritual—we often unconsciously or consciously force ourselves to.

Since our body, our mind and our spirit are all interconnected, having a healthy body can actually enhance our spirituality. Exercise increases the flow of what is known as prana, the energy that vitalizes all living things.

Prana is the Sanskrit word for "breath" or "breath of life." Prana is the life energy that vitalizes all living things and controls all activities in the body—physical and spiritual, mental and sensory. Without it, blood won't circulate, organs won't function and the brain won't do its job. In fact, some proponents of yoga believe that disease is due to an imbalance of prana and that sickness can be controlled when the proper flow of prana is restored.

A lack of prana can influence the mind and the emotions as well. Clinical tests have shown that there is a relationship between poor breathing and low IQ in children. And it's not hard to see how being confined to a stuffy room for too long can produce moodiness, depression or apathy—instead of the buoyancy that an energy boost of fresh air and prana will provide.

Prana is said to be most easily absorbed into the body through the air. As you exercise, especially in fresh air and sunshine, with each breath you are inhaling air charged with this dynamic force.

> *The human body is only vitality, energy, and spirit.... If you want to learn the Great Way, you must value the three treasures.*
>
> —LÜ YEN

Our exercise time can be a time for spiritual as well as physical renewal. We can use that time to go into our heart, attune with our Higher Self and send blessings to those in need. As we walk, we can say our prayers and affirmations. When I go for walks in the beautiful mountains of Montana, I like to breathe deeply, commune with God and nature, and offer my prayers.

Offering prayers while engaging in physical activity or work is an ancient practice. The Hindu text the Shiva-Purana, for instance, explains that the mantra to Shiva is effective "when repeated by a person whether walking or standing or doing any other work." And Mother Teresa tells us, "Work doesn't stop prayer, and prayer doesn't stop work."

In addition to your exercise breaks, longer periods of spiritual and physical renewal are essential. The key is to take time out—whether it's a yoga retreat or a long afternoon hike in the woods or by the ocean—*before* you reach your breaking point, the point where you become ineffective because you're out of balance.

Earlier I talked about the power of visualization to enhance our spiritual practices. What we visualize can be as powerful as what we do physically and emotionally to nourish our body, mind and soul. For example, we can employ the power of our inner vision to visualize ourselves filled with light.

Patanjali, the ancient compiler of the classic Yoga Sutra, taught, "Inner stability is gained by contemplating a luminous, sorrowless, effulgent light." One thirteenth-century Kabbalist advised, "Whatever one implants firmly in the mind becomes the essential thing. So if you pray and offer a blessing to God, or if you wish your intention to be true, imagine you are light. All around you—in every corner and on every side—is light.

> *Imagine you are light.*
> —A THIRTEENTH-CENTURY KABBALIST

"Turn to your right, and you will find shining light; to your left, splendor, a radiant light. Between them, up above, the light of the Presence. Surrounding that, the light of life.... This light is unfathomable and endless."[23]

Spiritual Exercises

■ **Assess your personal needs for renewal.** When you have the opportunity, do you allow yourself time for renewal before the next busy cycle hits?

How much time each week do you personally need for physical and spiritual renewal in order to maintain your balance and creativity?

■ **Make maximum use of your time for spiritual renewal.** Here are some simple mantras you can repeat as you are exercising, walking, driving, cooking or doing errands.

I AM a being of violet fire,
I AM the purity God desires!

Let God be magnified!

I AM the resurrection and the life of
*every cell and atom of my being**
now made manifest!

*You can replace the phrase "every cell and atom of my being" with whatever it is you want to energize, such as "my health," "my kidneys," "my relationship," "my business," "my finances."

■ **For a spiritual recharge, give the "I AM Light" exercise.** To enhance the flow of energy, sit in a comfortable position with your feet flat on the floor or your legs in a lotus posture.

Visualization:

Visualize your divine spark burning within your heart. See it expanding within your chest as a brilliant ball of white fire.

Then see your entire form sealed in a globe of white fire. See the white light strengthening first your body, then your emotions, then your mind. If your mind wanders, gently bring it back to your visualization of the white light.

When you are ready, recite the following affirmation, visualizing the light going forth from your heart as thousands of sunbeams to uplift, energize and heal those who need the light of your heart.

"I AM" is capitalized because each time you say, "I AM...," you are really affirming, "God in me is..." Whatever you affirm following the words "I AM" will become a reality, for the light of God flowing through you will obey that command.

I AM Light

I AM light, glowing light,
Radiating light, intensified light.
God consumes my darkness,
Transmuting it into light.

This day I AM a focus of the Central Sun.
Flowing through me is a crystal river,
A living fountain of light
That can never be qualified
By human thought and feeling.
I AM an outpost of the Divine.
Such darkness as has used me
    is swallowed up
By the mighty river of light which I AM.

I AM, I AM, I AM light.
I live, I live, I live in light.
I AM light's fullest dimension.
I AM light's purest intention.
I AM light, light, light
Flooding the world everywhere I move,
Blessing, strengthening and conveying
The purpose of the kingdom of heaven.

12 Work with a spiritual coach

*The blessing of the Guru [spiritual teacher]
is the most precious thing in life.*

—RAVI SHANKAR

When we want to master a new skill, we find someone who is accomplished in that field and become his or her student. We apprentice ourselves to a personal trainer, someone who has taken this road before and can teach us how to avoid the obstacles to the goal. This is no less true of our spiritual life, which has its own rigors and challenges as well as proven techniques for smoother sailing.

Many dismiss the need for a spiritual coach

(teacher/mentor) with "I can do it on my own, thank you." It's true that we all have to forge our own path and face our own tests along life's way. But it's also true that those who have already attained the same spiritual goals we aspire to can make the trek a lot easier. That's why the lives of the heroes and heroines of East and West have always been the fabric of fireside chats and the pull of popular movies. Our souls want to learn from those who have already arrived.

We can all use the help of a personal trainer to get fit spiritually, and the best trainers I know of are the ascended masters. They are coaches in the highest sense of the word.

"Ascended masters" is another name for the saints and adepts of East and West who have risen out of every culture and religion. They are called *ascended* masters because they have mastered the circumstances of life, overcome the human ego, fulfilled their life's purpose, graduated from earth's schoolroom and "ascended"—that is, accelerated in consciousness to become one with God. In Western religion we say they've entered heaven. In Eastern terms, they have become enlightened or attained parinirvana.

If there is one spiritual truth that is firmly rooted in the traditions of both East and West, it is that there are higher dimensions of reality "peopled with spiritual beings," as Mary Baker Eddy wrote. "Advancing spiritual steps in the teeming universe of Mind," she said, "lead on to spiritual spheres and exalted beings."[24] These "exalted beings" have each mastered a certain spiritual attribute, which they are supremely qualified to teach us—such as mercy, wisdom, compassion, faith, love, healing, charity, courage.

> *Hitch your wagon to a star.*
>
> —RALPH WALDO EMERSON

These advanced spiritual beings tutor and guide us at inner levels. While we will learn from many different teachers throughout our life, the ascended masters can lend an extraordinary helping hand (or more than one) to sponsor us in our field of endeavor. Their unparalleled spiritual impetus can help us master the art of practical spirituality and fulfill the divine plan of our life.

One important reason we can benefit from a spiritual coach is that we don't always see ourselves accurately. We don't see our own weaknesses, or if we do, we don't know how to overcome them.

Bodhidharma, the founder of Zen Buddhism in China and the martial art kung-fu, expressed it this way: "When mortals are alive, they worry about death. When they are full, they worry about hunger. Theirs is the Great Uncertainty. But sages do not consider the past. And they do not worry about the future. Nor do they cling to the present. And from moment to moment they follow the Way.

"If you have not awakened to this great truth, you had better look for a teacher on earth or in the heavens. Do not compound your own deficiency."[25]

Spiritual coaches do help us to overcome

our weak points, but they also help us develop and leverage our strong points. (Where would Luke Skywalker be without Obi-Wan Kenobi?) They inspire and guide us to become all that we are meant to be.

A teacher in the truest sense of the word wants you not only to match his or her attainment but to go beyond it. A real teacher is a facilitator who inspires the disciple to climb to the summit of his or her own being. That is the way some of the earliest Christians, known as gnostics,[26] saw Jesus.

The gnostic Gospel of Philip, for instance, describes the follower of Jesus as one who walks fully in his footsteps and is "no longer a Christian but a Christ." In the Gospel of Thomas, Jesus says, "He who will drink from my mouth will become as I am," and in the Secret Book of James he admonishes, "Become better than I."

Even in the New Testament Gospels, Jesus says, "Be ye therefore perfect, even as your Father which is in heaven is perfect" and "He that believeth on me, the works that I do shall he do also; and greater works than these shall he do, because I go unto my Father."[27]

Likewise, one Buddhist text says, "The Germ of Buddhahood exists in every living being. Therefore, forever and anon, all that lives is endowed with the Essence of the Buddha"—the potential to become the Buddha. The Zen master Hakuin Zenji simply said, "all beings by nature are Buddha, as ice by nature is water."

> Confucius was once asked about the way of good people. He replied, "If you do not walk in their footsteps, you do not gain access to their abode."

Of course, the end of the exercise is not just to gain spiritual mastery, peace or enlightenment for ourselves. As Mark Prophet once said, "Spiritual mastery means you are master of yourself first of all, and then you are able to assist other people—because you are able to manage and assist yourself. If you cannot take care of your own house and set your own house in order, how can you possibly help other people to set their house in order?"

How do you find your ascended master coach and how do you create a working relationship with him or her? Is there a saint or master you feel close to? Start there.

The book *Lords of the Seven Rays*[28] has been a good starting point for many to learn about the lives of seven masters who are very close to the souls of earth. These seven masters have volunteered to mentor our souls—to coach each one of us in what we personally need to accelerate our self-mastery and our practical spirituality.

Spiritual Exercises

■ **Walk and talk with your ascended master mentor.** Choose as a spiritual coach an ascended master you feel close to or admire, such as Jesus, Saint Francis, Confucius, Shiva, Gautama Buddha, Kuan Yin, Mary, Saint Germain. Start by studying his or her life. Ask yourself: *What was the primary virtue, the special spiritual quality he developed? How did she face the challenges of life?*

Most importantly, create a heart-tie with that master. Talk to her just as you would with a friend. Tell her when you need help.

Walk and talk with that master throughout the day. In any given situation ask the master: *"What would you do right now?"*

Don't stop knocking on that master's door until you get your answer. That answer may come as an inner prompting or feeling, as an outward sign reflected in events, or through someone's words—a "messenger" who enters your world.

■ **Study your master's special brand of practical spirituality.** Go through each of the keys to practical spirituality that you have read in this book and ask yourself how your master(s) exemplified these keys:

1 *How did they shape their soul's passion into a mission?*

2 *What were their priorities in life?*

3 *How did they stay attuned to the inner voice of wisdom, and what did they learn from that inner voice?*

4 *What helped them make a spiritual connection each day?*

5 *What techniques did they use to bring divine intercession into the world?*

6 *How did they express their spiritual nature, and what obstacles did they first need to clear out of the way?*

7 *How did they stay focused on the present?*

8 *What spiritual tools did they use to resolve their karma and foster their spiritual growth?*

9 *How did they turn every encounter and circumstance into an opportunity for spiritual growth?*

10 *How did they express their loving-kindness toward others—and toward themselves?*

11 *How did they deal with creative tension, and how did they renew themselves?*

12 *Who were their mentors, and what lessons did they learn from them?*

■ **Self-reflect.** After you have identified the virtues that helped your master navigate through the challenges of life, ask yourself what you need to do to develop those virtues.

Try to put their techniques into practice while experimenting with what your soul needs to soar to its own heights.

NOTES

1. The gnostics were those who belonged to a number of Christian sects that thrived in the early centuries of Christianity. Their teachings were later suppressed by the church. The gnostics claimed to possess the secret teachings of Jesus handed down from his closest disciples. Some scholars believe that some of the recorded teachings of the gnostics predate the New Testament Gospels and may more accurately represent Jesus' original teachings.

2. Karma is the law of cause and effect, the law of the circle. Karma is the effects of the causes we have set in motion in the past. See pages 94–97.

3. C. Norman Shealy and Caroline M. Myss, *The Creation of Health: The Emotional, Psychological, and Spiritual Responses That Promote Health and Healing* (Walpole, N.H.: Stillpoint Publishing, 1988, 1993), p.10.

Opening quotation to section 3: from *Hua Hu Ching: The Unknown Teachings of Lao Tzu,* by Brian Walker (HarperSanFrancisco, 1994), p. 36.

4. Adin Steinsaltz, *On Being Free* (Northvale, N.J.: Jason Aronson, 1995), pp. 235–36.

5. Swami Prabhavananda, trans., *Narada's Way of Divine Love (Narada Bhakti Sutras)* (Madras: Sri Ramakrishna Math, 1971), commentary on aphorism 5, pp. 30-31.

6. *Spiritual Testimonies* 48, in *The Collected Works of St. Teresa of Avila,* trans. Kieran Kavanaugh and Otilio Rodriguez (Washington, D.C.: ICS Publications, 1976), 1:344-45.

7. *The Book of Her Life* 26:2, in Kavanaugh and Rodriguez, *Collected Works of St. Teresa of Avila,* 1:171.

8. The Chart of Your Divine Self is described on pages 79–82. Color replicas of the Chart are available as posters (6" x 9" and 15" x 26") and wallet-size cards (2⅛" x 3⅝") from Summit University Press.

9. *The Book of Her Life* 8.5 and *The Way of Perfection* 26:9, in Kavanaugh and Rodriguez, *Collected Works of St. Teresa of Avila,* 1:67, 2:136.

10. To help you make the most of the moments available to you for your spiritual work, Elizabeth Clare Prophet has produced several tapes and

CDs of prayers, affirmations and mantras, published by Summit University Press.

11. Isa. 45:11; Job 22:27, 28.

12. See Elizabeth Clare Prophet, *How to Work with Angels,* published by Summit University Press.

13. Swami Prabhavananda, *Narada's Way of Divine Love,* p. 111.

14. Daniel Meacham, in William Safire and Leonard Safire, eds. and comps., *Words of Wisdom: More Good Advice* (New York: Simon and Schuster, 1989), p. 274.

15. Matt. 6:26, 28, 30.

16. Fritjof Capra, *The Tao of Physics,* 2d ed. (New York: Bantam Books, 1984), p. 141.

17. Dannion Brinkley, quoted in Elizabeth Clare Prophet with Patricia R. Spadaro and Murray L. Steinman, *Saint Germain's Prophecy for the New Millennium* (Corwin Springs, Mont.: Summit University Press, 1999), p. 305.

18. See *Spiritual Techniques to Heal Body, Mind and Soul,* 90-min. audiocassette published by Summit University Press. On this tape, Elizabeth Clare Prophet discusses the creative power of sound

and the violet flame and demonstrates dynamic techniques you can use to transform your personal life and bring spiritual solutions to today's global challenges.

19. See Elizabeth Clare Prophet, *Saint Germain's Prophecy for the New Millennium,* published by Summit University Press. Mrs. Prophet explores the most compelling prophecies for our time and shows how to use the violet flame to bring balance, harmony and positive change into our lives and mitigate the negative portents of prophecy.

20. See Surya Das, *The Snow Lion's Turquoise Mane: Wisdom Tales from Tibet* (HarperSanFrancisco, 1992), pp. 68–69.

21. Norman Rockwell, *Norman Rockwell: My Adventures as an Illustrator* (Garden City, N.Y.: Doubleday & Company, 1960), p. 351.

22. See Jack Kornfield and Christina Feldman, *Soul Food: Stories to Nourish the Spirit and the Heart* (HarperSanFrancisco, 1996), p. 134.

23. Daniel C. Matt, *God and the Big Bang: Discovering Harmony between Science and Spirituality* (Woodstock, Vt.: Jewish Lights Publishing, 1996), p. 73.

24. Mary Baker Eddy, *Science and Health with Key to the Scriptures* (Boston: First Church of Christ, Scientist, 1971), p. 513.

25. Red Pine, trans., *The Zen Teaching of Bodhidharma* (San Francisco: North Point Press, 1989), p. 75.

26. See note 1.

27. Matt. 5:48; John 14:12.

28. Mark L. Prophet and Elizabeth Clare Prophet, *Lords of the Seven Rays,* published by Summit University Press.

SUMMIT UNIVERSITY 🔥 PRESS®

Summit University Press books are available from fine
bookstores everywhere. For a free catalog or to place an
order, please call 1-800-245-5445 or 406-848-9500.

Karma and Reincarnation
Transcending Your Past, Transforming Your Future

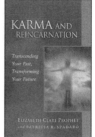

The word *karma* has made it into the mainstream. But not everyone understands what it really means or how to deal with it. This insightful book will help you come to grips with karmic connections from past lives that have helped create the circumstances of your life today. You'll discover how your actions in past lives—good and bad—affect which family you're born into, who you're attracted to, and why some people put you on edge. You'll learn about group karma, what we do between lives, and how to turn your karmic encounters into grand opportunities to shape the future you want.

ISBN: 0-922729-61-1
224 pages $6.95

Soul Mates and Twin Flames
The Spiritual Dimension of Love and Relationships

"After thirty-five years as a relationship counselor, I find *Soul Mates and Twin Flames* to be extremely powerful in revealing the inner mysteries of the soul and the true essence of love through its insightful analysis of real-life experiences and classical love stories."

—MARILYN C. BARRICK, Ph.D.,
author of *Sacred Psychology of Love*

ISBN: 0-922729-48-4
166 pages $5.95

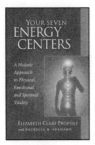

ISBN: 0-922729-56-5
234 pages $6.95

Your Seven Energy Centers
A Holistic Approach to Physical, Emotional and Spiritual Vitality

"What is so beautiful about this book is that it can speak to everyone about revitalization and inner peace."

—MAGICAL BLEND MAGAZINE

"Marries ancient healing wisdom with practical spiritual insights to help you create your own dynamic and uniquely personal healing journey. Your 21st-century guide to integrating and healing body, mind and soul."

—ANN LOUISE GITTLEMAN, author of *The Living Beauty Detox Program*

"A small book with a big message.... This handy little guide is packed with useful insights."

—WHOLE LIFE TIMES

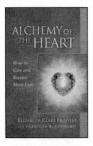

ISBN: 0-922729-60-3
204 pages $6.95

Alchemy of the Heart
How to Give and Receive More Love

"There is no way you can read this book and not feel more love for those around you—and as you do, you can see the healing changes that love will bring."

—MAGICAL BLEND MAGAZINE

"Through this 'pocket guide to practical spirituality' we learn the alchemical means to heal and empower our hearts, fulfill our reason for being, and extend our capacity to love. In other words, we learn how we can become 'a living transformer of love.'"

—BODHI TREE BOOK REVIEW

How to Work with Angels

"Angels—and our relationship to them—are neither a trend nor a fad....Ultimately, one's relationship with an angel is a personal one, and in *How to Work with Angels,* you'll discover how to make angels more present in your life.... Whether for love, healing, protection, guidance, or illumination, angels stand ready to help you in many practical and personal ways.... Also included here are a collection of visualizations, affirmations, prayers and decrees." —BODHI TREE BOOK REVIEW

ISBN: 0-922729-41-7
118 pages $5.95

Creative Abundance
Keys to Spiritual and Material Prosperity

"*Creative Abundance* contains keys for magnetizing the spiritual and material abundance we all need. Its sensible step-by-step techniques—including treasure mapping, principles of feng shui, meditations, visualizations and affirmations—show how to live a full and prosperous life."

—BODHI TREE BOOK REVIEW

ISBN: 0-922729-38-7
174 pages $5.95

SUMMIT UNIVERSITY PRESS®

Available at fine bookstores everywhere
or call 1-800-245-5445.

FOR MORE INFORMATION

Summit University Press books
are available at fine bookstores worldwide
and at your favorite on-line bookseller.
Our books are translated into over 15 languages.
If you would like to receive a free catalog
featuring our books and products,
please contact

SUMMIT UNIVERSITY ☙ PRESS®
PO Box 5000
Corwin Springs, MT 59030-5000 USA

1-800-245-5445 or 406-848-9500

Fax 1-800-221-8307 or 406-848-9555

E-mail: info@summituniversitypress.com

Web site: www.summituniversitypress.com

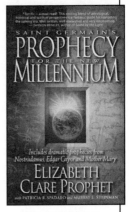